In 1965-66, the Israeli government pursued a policy designed to bring about a recession in the economy, with the object of reducing the country's rate of inflation and its balance of payments deficit. Mrs Greenwald has provided the only comprehensive and systematic study on this subject. First it analyzes the policy, showing how Israel's economic, social and political structure influenced its choice of monetary, fiscal and other measures. It then assesses the effectiveness of these measures and of the policy as a whole. The slowing down of the rise in prices and reduction of the balance of payments deficit are related to the past and hypothetical future trends. And, using input-output tables and other statistical techniques, the structural changes induced by the recession are examined: to what extent were resources shifted from the domestic market to the export sector? How far was import-substitution accelerated? These and other related questions are raised and tested.

The book draws on much unpublished material in Hebrew and English. Its scholarship is of the highest order, and it is clearly and concisely written. It will appeal not only to those interested in Israel's economics and politics but to the much larger number concerned with macro-economic problems and the effectiveness of government stabilization measures.

THE AUTHOR. Carol Schwartz Greenwald, who gained her Ph.D. at Columbia University, was appointed Assistant Vice-President of the Federal Reserve Bank, Boston, Massachusetts, at the end of 1972.

Volume 5
THE MODERN MIDDLE EAST SERIES
sponsored by
The Middle East Institute
Columbia University, New York

Recession as a
Policy Instrument
Israel 1965–1969
by
CAROL SCHWARTZ GREENWALD

Rutherford · Madison · Teaneck
Fairleigh Dickinson University Press

© 1973, The Middle East Institute
Columbia University, New York

First American edition published 1973 by
Associated University Presses, Inc.,
Cranbury, New Jersey 08512.

Library of Congress Catalogue Card Number: 73-2895

ISBN 0-8386-1396-9
Printed in Great Britain

PREFACE

Among the economic problems of developing countries, controlling inflation and expanding exports are two of the most important. This study explores the experience of one developing country, Israel, in applying the traditional techniques of monetary and fiscal policies to these problems. Inflation and trade problems are analyzed as business cycle as well as economic development phenomena.

This study examines the effectiveness of a recession in Israel during the mid-1960s as a policy instrument in restructuring production toward exports and in halting an inflationary spiral. Israel's domestic economic policies are surveyed in the light of her balance of trade position, with attention focused on the domestic adjustments which facilitated or hindered the attainment of external balance. The analysis indicates that the recession did induce structural changes which allowed Israel to renew rapid growth with an industrial structure more aligned to its development needs. Input-output techniques were used to determine the extent to which the decline in residential construction led to a shifting of real resources from construction to industry, furthering the goal of export-led growth.

The effectiveness of an economic recession in combating inflation or in fundamentally altering a trade balance has been the subject of much controversy in recent years. The view has become increasingly popular that the use of incomes policies and devaluations have done away with the need for deflationary monetary and fiscal policies. The Israeli experience not only indicates the usefulness of restrictive policies in trade adjustments under inflationary conditions, it also illustrates the essentially supplementary nature of incomes policies and devaluations in this kind of economic environment. This is clearly shown by the comparisons of Israel's experience with incomes policies and devaluations when used alone and when employed in conjunction with a recession.

I am happy to acknowledge the aid I have received from many persons at different stages of this work. I am deeply grateful to Professor Charles Issawi and Professor J. C. Hurewitz, without whose advice and efforts this book could never have been completed.

I also wish to thank Professor Peter Kenen, Professor Zvi Ankori and Professor Albert Hart for their perceptive criticisms of the original manuscript. I am also indebted to Mr. David Schwartz of the Israeli Treasury and Mr. Eliezer Sheffer of the Bank of Israel for their patience during numerous interviews in explaining facets of the Israeli economy to me and their help in arranging meetings with other Israeli economists and government officials.

Miss Linda Gray was my energetic research assistant. Mrs. Judy Liss helped with the proofs and compiled the index. Miss Susan Smith cheerfully typed the many versions of this manuscript. I am very grateful for their help.

I sincerely thank my husband, Ronald, for his understanding and for his patience during the endless evenings and weekends that I worked on this thesis. I am deeply indebted to my mother, Dorothy Schwartz, for her constant encouragement during my studies.

CONTENTS

Page

Preface   v

Part I The Background of Israeli Economic Policy

I. The Importance of Trade Adjustment   3
Methods of Trade Adjustment   4
Israeli Economic Policies   8

II. The Institutional Setting   12
Fiscal Policy   12
The Budget   12
Balance of Payments   14
Incomes   15
Monetary Policy   17

Part II Israeli Economic Policies in the 1960s

Introduction: Policy Goals and Accomplishments   25

III. The Boom and the Recession   28
Restraining the Boom: 1964–1965   28
Monetary Policy   28
Fiscal Policy   32
The Recession: 1966–1967   35
Fiscal Policy   35
Monetary Policy   38
The Trade Balance: 1965–1967   41
Imports   41
Exports   41

IV. The Economic Upturn: 1967–1969   51
Monetary Policy   51
Fiscal Policy   55
The Budget and Defense Spending   55
Export Promotion   57
Incomes Policy   59
Renewed Attempts at Budgetary Restraint   59

The Trade Balance   60
    Imports   60
    Exports   61
    Appendix: Imports and Exports of Services   68

Part III Internal Adjustments to Israeli Economic Policies

V. The Residential Construction Sector   77
    Public Housing and Immigration   78
    The Private Housing Market: 1962–1969   78
    The Building Recession   82
        Causes   82
        Effects: An Input-Output Analysis   88

VI. The Industrial Sector   96
    The Structural Background   96
    The Role of the Development Budget   103
    The Cycle in Private Business Investment   105
    The Effects of the Recession   112
        Wages, Prices, and Productivity   112
        Industrial Structure   116

VII. Private Consumption and an Incomes Policy   129
    The Government's Incomes Policies and
        Consumption: 1964–1969   130
    The Effectiveness of Israel's Incomes Policy   136

VIII. Conclusion: Policy Alternatives   140

Bibliography   145

LIST OF TABLES

Chapter		Title	Page
2.	1.	Sources of Growth in Financial Assets	13
	2.	An International Comparison of Imports and Exports as a Proportion of GNP	14
	3.	Reserve Requirements and Banks' Balance Sheets When Loaned to Capacity	19
	4.	Bank Credit	20
3.	1.	Summary of Monetary Policy Actions	29
	2.	The Money Supply, Quarterly	30
	3.	The Money Supply	31
	4.	Bank Credit	32
	5.	Summary of Government Budgets	34
	6.	Sources of Growth in Financial Assets	39
	7.	A Comparison of Industrial Production and Industrial Exports	46
4.	1.	The Money Supply	51
	2.	Sources of Growth in Financial Assets	52
	3.	Summary of Monetary Policy Actions	53
	4.	Summary of Government Budgets	56
	5.	Expected Values of Commodity Imports, Exports, and the Commodity Trade Surplus Compared to Actual Values	65
	6.	Measures of Economic Dependence	67
		Appendix: 1A The Current Account	69
		2A Net Imports and Exports of Services: 1965–1969	70
5.	1.	GNP, Net Immigration and Public Housing	80 and 81

Chapter			Page
	2.	Change in the Relative Position of the Construction Industry in the Israeli Economy	85
	3.	Industries Which Supply Inputs to the Residential Construction Sector	90
	4.	Industries Which Supply Inputs Either Directly or Indirectly to the Residential Construction Sector	91
	5.	Effects of the Decline in Residential Construction on Other Economic Sectors	92
	6.	A Comparison of the Actual Change in Gross Industrial Output with that Induced By Changes in Residential Construction and Exports: 1965–1968	93
6.	1.	Average Rate of Customs Duty Per Main Branch	99
	2.	Gross Fixed Non-Dwelling Investment	104
	3.	Foreign Transfers to the Public Sector	106
	4.	Net Loans Granted by the Public Sector	107
	5.	Investment in Machinery and Equipment	108
	6.	Wage Increases in Israel and in Israel's Major Export Markets	113
	7.	Unit Labor Costs in Israel and Developed Industrial Countries	114
	8.	Increases in Consumer Prices in Israel and in Other Industrial Countries	117
	9.	Distribution of Real Industrial Output and Growth of Exports	120
	10.	Increase in Industrial Output Stemming from Changes in Final Demand	121
	11.	Distribution of Real Industrial Output	124 and 125
7.	1.	Estimated and Actual Money Wage Rate Increases in Israel: 1957–1969	137

CHARTS

Chapter   Page

3.   1.   Total Commodity Imports   42
     2.   Imports and Industrial Production   43
     3.   Consumer Goods Imports and Unemployment   44
     4.   Commodity Exports   47
     5.   Industrial Exports   48

4.   1.   Imports and Industrial Production   62
     2.   Commodity Exports   63
     3.   Industrial Exports   64

5.   1.   Net Immigration, Real GNP and Public
              Housing Construction   79
     2.   Residential Building Area Started   83
     3.   Indicators of Construction Activity   86

6.   1.   Commercial and Industrial Building   109
     2.   Productivity, Wages and Unit Labor Costs   111
     3.   Prices   115
     4.   Industrial Production and Industrial
              Employment   119
     5.   Distribution of Real Industrial Output by
              Type of Production   123
     6.   Proportion of Industrial Output Allocated
              to Exports   126

PART I

The Background of
Israeli Economic Policy

CHAPTER I

THE IMPORTANCE OF TRADE ADJUSTMENT

In a classical setting of flexible prices and wages, deflationary monetary and fiscal policies will remedy a balance of trade deficit without creating prolonged unemployment. If wages and prices are flexible, then a decrease in aggregate demand induced by the deflationary policies will lower both wages and prices. Prices and output of goods sold in the domestic market will be hardest hit by the induced decrease in domestic demand. Goods produced for the export market will become more attractive to producers, since their prices depend upon the state of demand elsewhere and will not be pulled down by the domestic decline in demand. Exporters will benefit from the slackened demand situation in the domestic market by being able to employ labor at the lower wage rates now prevalent in the economy, thus increasing both the profitability and the output of exports. If the economy has previously been at full employment, the reduced level of domestic demand will enable exporters to obtain additional factors of production (which are now unemployed) without bidding up their prices, making it possible for them to increase the volume of their exports. In short, deflationary policies will remedy a balance of trade deficit by lowering domestic prices and wages (making exports more and imports less attractive) and by shifting resources into export-oriented production.

In the modern world of price and wage rigidities, economic adjustment tends to focus initially on employment and output. Slowed economic growth or a recession leads first to declines in employment and output, which reduce incomes and cut the demand for imports, indeed for all goods. As unsold goods pile up and capacity utilization rates fall, exports become more attractive, since they now only have to cover marginal costs to be worthwhile.

This adjustment is aided by relative price movements. In a world of constantly rising prices, a recession at home will slow domestic prices relative to price increases abroad. An absolute deflation, like that brought about in the classical system, is not necessary to improve a competitive trade position as long as this relative slowing occurs. The reduction in aggregate spending can thus "lower" domestic prices and cause both the substitution of home goods for

3

imports in the "deflating" country and the substitution of its exports for foreign goods in markets abroad. Such substitution will help to restore balance, provided the sum of home and foreign price elasticities of demand for imports exceeds unity.[1]

Any nation may find a recession necessary to break inflationary expectations which have resulted in an inflationary wage-price spiral, nonproductive investments and reduced savings; to reorient producers' thinking away from meeting domestic demands and toward export markets and, at the same time, to release the necessary real resources for export production; or to reduce spending from previously inflated levels based on borrowed money to levels more appropriate to the nation's real income. In examining the effects of the recession of the mid-1960's on the structure of the Israeli economy and on the balance of trade, my major analytic emphasis will be on the domestic linkages which either facilitated or hindered the desired adjustments toward higher exports and lowered imports. The structural changes induced in the economy's output mix allowed Israel to renew rapid growth with an industrial structure more aligned to its development needs. A decline in the importance of residential construction and a shifting of real resources from construction furthered the rapid expansion of exports. In addition, sharply higher defense spending after the Six-Day War promoted industrial growth both by increasing the domestic demand for industrial products and by creating and expanding military industries, whose products also provided new exports.

Extending the analysis through 1969, I shall note which changes were maintained during Israel's period of rapid economic expansion. The post-recession period also offers an opportunity to investigate why a devaluation and export subsidies were successful in expanding exports, whereas they would not have been prior to 1967.

Emphasis will be placed on the political setting in which all economic decisions must be made. Since inflation and consequent trade deficits became widespread after World War II, a detailed examination of the effects of deflationary policies on the Israeli economy should shed some light on the potential usefulness of the classical medicine in a world of price and wage rigidities.

Methods of Trade Adjustment

A devaluation is usually proposed as the means to narrow a trade deficit. Restrictive domestic policies, however, must also be employed if the economy is at full employment. In a fully employed economy a devaluation without accompanying restrictive measures would foster inflation, while deflationary measures alone would solve the economy's payments problem at the expense of higher unemployment. When a devaluation is needed to maintain the level of aggregate demand, it must be coupled with sufficient deflation to release goods for export and import substitution. Deflationary measures prevent the demand shifts resulting from devaluation from producing an inflation which would nullify the effects of a devaluation. The Israeli devaluation of 1962 was unsuccessful partly because domestic policies did not effect sufficient "disabsorption," whereas the devaluation of 1967, took place when there was sufficient slack in the economy to eliminate the need for "disabsorption."

Deflation

In an economy which is suffering from "over-full" employment – an economy in external and internal imbalance – devaluation is worse than useless; deflationary measures alone must be relied upon to aid the attainment of external balance both by changing relative prices and by affecting output. Restrictive measures make imports relatively more expensive compared to home goods. If export prices are determined by foreign demand and supply conditions – that is, if the deflating country is a price taker in its export markets – then the fact that export prices will not have fallen while the prices of home goods will have, increases the attractiveness of exports. Deflationary policies, by reducing aggregate demand, also release real resources for import substitution and exports. If the economy were over-fully employed, the decrease in aggregate demand would reduce inflationary pressures but would not cause enduring unemployment. Unemployment would temporarily be higher as shifts in employment would probably lag behind the induced shifts in demand. This was the situation which Israeli policymakers believed they faced in 1964 when they decided on a slowdown policy without an accompanying devaluation.

Deflationary financial policies can promote balance of payments adjustments by their direct effects on interest rates and the availability of funds and by their indirect effects on domestic expenditures. The indirect effects are the most applicable to the Israeli economy because until 1970 Israel had a maximum interest rate set by law which was below the prevailing market rate of interest, so that the Bank of Israel was unable to use variations in interest rates as a policy instrument. Furthermore, since Israel is not a major financial center, it is doubtful whether much foreign short-term capital would be attracted to it even if interest rates did rise. The main effect of deflationary policies, therefore, had to be on domestic spending. To the extent that the decrease in demand pressures is directed toward import (or export) goods, the balance of trade will be immediately affected. Even that part of the decreased spending that is directed to home goods other than exports will in time affect the balance of trade, for the lower expenditures will tend to lower prices, and lower domestic prices may decrease the proportion of aggregate spending directed to import goods.

Deflationary measures act on aggregate expenditure by reducing home consumption and investment of imported and domestic goods. There may be some increase in exports if the economy has been unable to satisfy demand from abroad. The deflationary measures will, of course, reduce production unless exports absorb the resources set free by the reduction in home demand. The net effect of these measures in improving the trade balance will be equal to the increase in exports plus the decrease in imports.

Subotnik used a model of the Israeli economy to simulate the results of a devaluation without offsetting monetary and fiscal policy actions. He found that the beneficial effect of devaluation on the balance of payments very quickly vanishes and soon becomes detrimental.

> But the reason for this rather surprising result can be easily found.... We see that the current effect of devaluation on current consumption of all kinds is relatively high [i.e., stimulates consumption because of the strong income effect]. But current consumption has a negative effect on the next year's exports (of all kinds) and a positive effect on the next year's imports (of all kinds), causing the balance of payments in the next year to deteriorate.[2]

In addition to raising consumption because of the strong income effect, a devaluation will increase current consumption in Israel because factor earnings (wages, interest, rents – everything but profits) are tied to the cost of living.

The peculiar character of collective bargaining in Israel adds a structural element which tends to defeat a devaluation. The fact that one labor union with political status (Histadrut) represents most of the nation's workers and really bargains with the government, not employers, has at least two negative effects for maintaining economic balance. First, virtually all labor earnings change at the same time, eliminating the lag found in other economies where many labor groups bargain separately and at different times. And since all Histadrut contracts are tied to the cost of living, all wages rise soon after prices rise. Secondly, politics rather than economics is often the prevailing consideration in bargaining. Workers identify their wage claims not with what their particular employer can afford to pay, but with what the government says the economy can afford, and the government's analysis of what the economy can afford is, in turn,

6

often influenced by the proximity of national elections.

When a devaluation increases the domestic currency receipts of export sales, the domestic producer finds this equivalent to a rise in the price of the goods he sells. Since the profit-maximizing level of output is higher, he will increase his output of export goods. In most economies, devaluation can thus offset shifts in marginal cost curves caused by higher wages. In Israel, however, a devaluation will be largely offset by the almost perfect adjustment of wages, though it occurs with a time lag.

If credit is not expanded freely, then higher unemployment will reduce domestic absorption despite cost-of-living adjustments for employed factors. Rising unemployment will also probably affect wage demands and make labor less insistent on a complete adjustment to higher prices. It is this slowing of the wage-price spiral that makes it imperative that credit be restricted. As Michaely points out:

> The coefficients of adjustment cannot in actual fact be taken as *given*: They are dependent on the *state of unemployment*. Thus the curb on credit may well slow down the wage-price spiral. The coefficients of adjustment may also depend on the state of *expectations*. Knowledge that the money supply is not allowed to expand will induce the belief that the price level is going to be relatively stable (even though, in effect, the restrictions on credit may actually bring unemployment rather than price stability). This belief in itself may *reduce* the coefficients of adjustment.[3]

Smithies draws the same conclusions about the need for restrictive policies.

> For the devaluation to be effective, domestic demand must be contracted correspondingly.... Failure to apply the required doses of classical medicine leads to further devaluation.... Consequently, I conclude that devaluation cannot be regarded as a substitute for fiscal and monetary discipline, although it can make that discipline more palatable.[4]

As in a recession, a reduction in economic welfare occurs when import controls are used. Since citizens cannot buy some of the goods they desire, real welfare is lower. Moreover, it is unlikely that a democratic country with a free enterprise economy will be able to rely on a comprehensive system of controls to contain excess demands indefinitely. With strong demand pressures, controls must be multiplied and enforcement becomes increasingly difficult.

Export subsidies have effects similar to those of devaluation. If they are not combined with import duties, import controls, or restrictive monetary and fiscal policies, then the higher income

7

generated by higher exports will be inflationary and raise import demands. When Evans used his econometric model of the Israeli economy to test the implications of a policy of export subsidization without offsetting restrictive domestic policies, he found

> that the subsidization of exports leads not only to a decrease in the net foreign balance but to an actual decline in exports as well. The new jobs created lead to higher prices, and other producers switch from the export to the domestic market. This agrees with policies which call for domestic slowdowns at the time of devaluations or other moves aimed at increasing the net foreign balance.[5]

Simulations done by Subotnik also indicated that subsidies on exports had a detrimental effect on the balance of payments because of the strong income effect.[6] Devaluation and direct controls also require restrictive monetary and fiscal policies, but even with these expedients, demand pressures in the economy must be reduced if a lasting effect is to be made on the trade balance.

Israeli Economic Policies

Poor in natural resources, Israel has needed extensive and varied imports. Imports constituted an average of 31 percent of the gross national product during the years 1950–9, rising to an average of 35 percent in the period 1960–4.[7] The overwhelming importance of imports in the Israeli economy is quite clear when Israel is compared with Great Britain, another resource-poor country noted for its dependence on raw-material imports. In 1968, Great Britain imported 21 percent of the goods and services she consumed or exported.[8]

Because of her dependence on imports, Israel must be dependent on export markets. During most of the past twenty years Israel has relied on a few products to earn much of her foreign exchange. Diamonds and citrus exports comprised 50 percent of commodity exports between the mid-1950's and the mid-1960's. The share of exports in total output, however, has been rising, from 7.2 percent of gross national product in the period 1950–64 to 19.6 percent in the period 1965–7.[9] In 1968 industrial exports accounted for 41 percent of the output of mining and quarrying, 18 percent of the output of textiles, 16 percent of the output of the chemicals and petroleum industry and 15 percent of the output of the clothing industry.[10]

Since exports averaged less than half the import ratio during this period, Israel has been dependent on foreign capital inflows to cover her large deficit on current account. Over the period 1949–65

8

unilateral transfers – mainly German reparations and restitution payments and contributions from world Jewry – financed over 70 percent of the import surplus with the remaining 30 percent financed mainly by long-term capital loans. Purchases of State of Israel bonds, primarily by world Jewry, accounted for almost 70 percent of long-term capital loans received during this period.[11] Israel's extreme dependence on capital inflows made her vulnerable to any changes which might reduce them.

From 1955 to 1964 capital flows were generally large enough to cover the trade deficit and to increase reserves. The Israeli government was free, therefore, to pursue a policy of rapid economic development and to allow a rapid rise in per capita private consumption. During this period real GNP rose at a rate of 10 percent annually, while investment grew at a rate of 11 percent and per capita private consumption at 5 percent. Inflation was a persistent problem, with prices rising at an average annual rate of 6.5 percent. The deficit on current account rose from $285 million to $570 million.[12]

The preoccupation of Israeli governments and economists with trade and payments problems, especially with the international ramifications of domestic policies, is understandable in view of Israel's dependence upon world trade. Devaluation, import controls, export subsidies, and recessionary policies have been used to move closer toward balanced trade. Import controls and export subsidies were most heavily relied on up to 1962, in a deliberate attempt to enable the government to pursue an economic development policy of rapid growth. By the period 1958–1962, when the economy had reached full employment, the system of controls had become so complex as to be unworkable. As described by Rubner, the system of controls finally led to the abdication of the Israeli pound as a standard of value.[13]

In 1962 the New Economic Policy was initiated. It combined a sharp devaluation of the Israeli pound (from IL = 55¢ to IL = 33¢) with the dismantling of direct import controls and a sharp reduction in the use of export subsidies. However, the government maintained its commitment to full employment and rapid growth. It hoped that an incomes policy and moral suasion would prevent inflationary pressures from undermining the devaluation.[14] In 1964 Israel experienced a trade deficit 28 percent greater than that in the previous year. The failure of government policies to ensure that the devaluation meant lower absorption doomed the devaluation.

In late 1964 the government accepted the position that it had to slow the rise of the Israeli standard of living. It did not, however, embark on a "slowdown" policy until after the October 1965 elections. By that time the economy itself had begun to slow as a

9

result of lower immigration and the end of a speculative construction boom. In line with its commitment to slow the economy's growth rate, the government undertook no action to offset these recessionary forces. Through most of 1966 it stuck to its resolve to "sacrifice" internal balance for external goals.

In fact, Israel could not continue her economic development policies if she were faced with a decline in foreign capital flows, especially of unilateral transfers. Such a decline began when restitution payments from Germany fell from $134 million in 1964 to $113 million in 1965. At the same time, German reparations, which had been $47 million in 1962, declined to $25 million in 1964 and to $22 million in 1965 and were to terminate entirely in early 1966. Net foreign investments in Israel also dropped from $143 million in 1964 to $83 million in 1965.[15]

These adverse capital movements, which forced a heavier reliance on expensive short-term loans, undermined the basis of past policies: rapid economic development financed by a large import surplus. The Bank of Israel stated that the required improvement in the balance of payments

...calls for a policy of restraining the expansion of disposable income and a greater effort to step up private and public saving and to stimulate exports. Foregoing an exaggerated rise in living standards in the present is the price that must be paid to achieve an even greater rise in the long run.[16]

The Finance Minister, Pinchas Sapir, expressed the same views in his 1966/67 Budget Address, which stated that at this point in Israel's development, rapid growth was not as important as a better trade balance. He warned that without an economic slowdown, the economy would return to the grim days of the early 1950's.[17]

10

1. J.E. Meade, *The Theory of International Economic Policy*, Vol. 1: *The Balance of Payments* (Cambridge, England: Oxford University Press, 1951), Chapter VI.

2. Abraham Subotnik, *The Development of an Econometric Model for Policy Decision-Making in Israel* unpublished Ph. D. dissertation, Department of Economics, Cornell University, 1967, pp. 179–80.

3. Michael Michaely, "Devaluation, Cost of Inflation, and the Supply of Exports", *Economia Internazionale*, IX (February 1956), p. 58.

4. Arthur Smithies, "The Balance of Payments and the Classical Medicine," *Review of Economics and Statistics*, XLVI (May 1964), p. 111.

5. Michael K. Evans, *An Econometric Model of Part of the Israeli Economy* (Discussion Paper No. 86; Philadelphia: University of Pennsylvania), p. 57.

6. Subotnik, *op cit.*, p. 184.

7. Economic Planning Authority, *Israel Economic Development, Past Progress and Plan for the Future* (Jerusalem, March 1968), p. 133.

8. International Monetary Fund (hereafter IMF). *International Financial Statistics* (Washington, D.C., May 1970), p. 322.

9. Economic Planning Authority, *loc. cit.*

10. Bank of Israel, *Annual Report 1968*, p. 260.

11. Nadav Halevi and Ruth Klinov-Malul, *The Economic Development of Israel* (New York: Frederick A. Praeger, 1968), pp. 157–8.

12. Economic Planning Authority, *op cit.*, p. 4. After adjustment for changes in the level of defense imports, the deficit in current account rose from $247 million to $471 million.

13. See Alex Rubner, *The Economy of Israel: A Critical Account of the First Ten Years* (New York: Frederick A. Praeger, 1960), for an analysis of the economic inefficiencies of this system.

14. See Miriam Beham, *Monetary Aspects of the 1962 Devaluation* (The Maurice Falk Institute for Economic Research in Israel; Jerusalem, October 1968) and Paul Gaebelein, Jr., "Devaluation Under Full Employment and Inflation: The Case of Israel", Unpublished Ph. D. dissertation, Department of Economics, Claremont Graduate School, 1967.

15. Data from Bank of Israel, *Annual Report 1968*, pp. 70–1. Data for 1962 from Halevi and Klinov-Malul, *op cit.* p. 295.

16. Bank of Israel, *Annual Report 1964*, p. 9. David Horowitz, Governor of the Bank of Israel, told me that he writes the first chapter in the Bank's *Annual Reports* and that the statements in this chapter can, therefore, be taken as his personal views.

17. *The Jerusalem Post*, February 15, 1966, p. 1.

CHAPTER II

THE INSTITUTIONAL SETTING
FOR MONETARY AND FISCAL POLICIES

Fiscal Policy

In Israel the share of resources used by or channeled through the public sector exceeds that in most market economies. In 1965 it accounted for about 28 percent of GNP. The importance of public sector operations resulted largely from the need to build infrastructure and to absorb a large number of immigrants, with heavy defense requirements adding further expenses.

A notable feature of the Israeli budget has been the large share provided by foreign sources of revenue, including German reparations, contributions from world Jewry, and external borrowing. A substantial share of the government's development expenditure is granted as credits, and a large portion of these funds comes from abroad. The government thus functions to some extent as a financial intermediary, receiving foreign funds and channeling them to domestic investment. Its budget actually understates the role of the public sector, since it does not include spending by the Jewish Agency, which finances many social and economic projects, especially those connected with immigrant absorption, which in other nations would be provided by the government.

The Budget

The proposed state budget for each fiscal year (April 1 to March 31), which indicates the Israeli government's economic plans for the coming year, is usually divided into an ordinary and a development section. Among the ordinary expenditures are government services, defense, subsidies, transfer payments, and interest on government debt. Development expenditures include investments, grants and loans for development, and debt retirement. Ordinary receipts encompass direct and indirect taxes and other obligatory payments. Capital receipts include unilateral transfers from abroad, foreign and domestic loans, and receipts from the sale of property and loan collection.

Two separate concepts are involved here. One is that current

12

Table 1. SOURCES OF GROWTH IN FINANCIAL ASSETS

	Growth in Financial Assets (IL Millions)	Percent Change in Financial Assets Due to Changes in				
		Accumulation of Foreign Currency Assets	Expansion of Credit to the Public*	Expansion of Credit to the Government	Other Factors, Including Open-Market Operations	Total
1964	254	16.5	58.3	37.4	-12.5	100.0
1965	394	55.6	34.5	14.0	-4.1	100.0
1966	408	-17.2	72.8	46.3	-2.0	100.0
1967	1,473	45.4	35.2	23.6	-4.1	100.0
1968	1,338	-12.9	44.1	72.8	-4.0	100.0
1969	983	-109.8	56.7	142.7	10.4	100.0

*Includes rediscounts and loans from the Bank of Israel.

SOURCE: Bank of Israel, Annual Reports.

13

government expenditure should be financed from current receipts. The second is concerned with the inflationary aspects of government finance:

> The division between the two parts of the budget reflects the widely held view that regular Government services should be financed from orthodox, non-inflationary sources, such as taxes and the sale of service, whereas development can be financed from loans as well, preferably long-term ones.[1]

In considering its indirect monetary implications, however, the source and type of loan are much more important than whether it is used for current or capital expenditure. Crucial factors are the total government debt financing and whether the debt diverts existing funds or creates new money. As Table 1 shows, deficit financing in the public sector has been a major expansionary force on the economy in most years.

Table 2. AN INTERNATIONAL COMPARISON OF IMPORTS AND EXPORTS AS A PROPORTION OF GNP (1965)

Country	Imports* as % of GNP	Exports* as % of GNP
Holland	45.1	44.6
Denmark	31.1	29.8
New Zealand	24.9	22.2
Switzerland	30.3	30.2
Israel	32.5	19.2

*Goods and services.

SOURCE: International Monetary Fund, International Financial Statistics (Washington, D. C., May 1970), country pages.

Balance of Payments Policy

Israel's trade problem reflects her low level of exports rather than a disproportionately high level of imports, as Table 2 shows. During most years the official foreign exchange rate of the Israeli pound has been above the market rate, and the government has manipulated exchange rates and other financial inducements to reduce the excess demand for foreign exchange and to encourage the development of exports and import substitutes. Until 1962 an important element in this policy was the system of multiple exchange rates and quotas on imports. The liberalization policy initiated in 1962 resulted in a unified exchange rate and, by 1965, in the virtual disappearance of administrative restrictions on imports. The latter were replaced by tariff restrictions.

Since 1965 the Government's import policy has been characterized by high, although declining, rates of tariff protection and continuous efforts to stimulate import substitutes directly. Thus, a major criterion for both development loans and approval for strong Government financial assistance has been whether the investment would produce import substitutes or exports.

To promote exports, the development of export industries has been aided by government loans and investments made through the development budget. To further export sales, the government has participated in funds to provide short-term credits for exporters and organized conferences which bring foreign businessmen into contact with their Israeli counterparts. Export subsidies were increasingly used as a substitute for devaluation from 1966 to 1969.

Incomes Policy

The European background of the early settlers and the sociopolitical conditions in Palestine led to the politicizing of all economic and social relationships. Kibbutzim, labor unions, workers' cooperatives, and commercial ventures were all undertaken by political parties. Individuals in each group were members of the same political party; if an individual's political views change, he would shift to a different kibbutz, union, etc. The parties were thus ideological groupings, not conglomerates of different interest groups, with their own economic bases.

When Histadrut was founded in 1920 as an umbrella organization for the economic undertakings of all parties, the political nature of the original ventures was transferred to it. The political parties present lists of candidates for all Histadrut posts, from local union steward to Secretary-General of Histadrut, and members vote for their party's list, not for individuals. Thus the power structure of Histadrut reflects the strength of the different political parties. For example, just as Mapai is the dominant member of the present coalition governing Israel, its members hold the dominant positions within Histadrut.

15

Histadrut was set up, not as a labor union, but as a political-economic institution with the utopian purpose of creating a new worker-oriented society. As such, it founded kibbutzim, organized businesses to employ Jewish labor, established a workers' school system and a national health organization and represented the urban workers through labor unions. The anomoly of Histadrut is shown by the fact that it is at once Israel's largest "private" employer and the labor union which represents most Israeli workers.

Bargaining between the government and Histadrut over wages is a complicated affair. To a certain extent, Histadrut acts like a company union, since both the government and Histadrut leaders have been chosen by the same political constituency. If a Histadrut executive were too independent of his party's position, he would not be placed on the party's list in the next election.

If there were a majority party in Israel, there would be little bargaining, since both the government and Histadrut would present the same party platforms. But Israel has a coalition government, and compromises must therefore be worked out. The nature of Israeli politics usually leads to large wage increases. Mapai, in order to retain the votes of the left-wing Mapam Party in government decisions, is largely forced to agree to Mapam's wage demands in formulating agreements with Histadrut. The balance is further tilted toward large wage increases because Mapai is afraid of losing votes if it allows Mapam to appear as the workers' champion.

The bargaining process takes place in four stages. First each political party determines its own national wage policy position. Then the government officials meet with Histadrut executives. Histadrut presents the wage decisions to the Manufacturers Association, which represents private industrial employers. The Manufacturers Association has little bargaining leverage, however, for not only has the government already agreed to support the wage proposals, but the country's largest "private" employer — Histadrut — has already accepted them. The most effective bargaining position the private employers have is to demand increased government subsidies to offset the higher wage costs, which they cannot "afford." This may put pressure on the government to force Histadrut to moderate its wage demands, because the government cannot afford the politically unpopular measure of raising taxes to give subsidies to employers.

A new final stage of bargaining recently grew out of a reaction against Histadrut's policy of equalizing wages for all skill levels. The highly educated rejected Histadrut as their bargaining agent in order to regain larger wage differentials between skill groups. The engineers and academicians, who are largely on government payrolls, bargain directly with the government, usually for wage increases larger than those gained by Histadrut. Again, the importance of votes vies with budget deficits in determining the final outcome.

The fact that all Histadrut labor contracts call for adjusting wages to changes in the cost of living has accelerated price and wage increases and impeded effective anti-inflationary measures, including devaluations. A devaluation usually attempts to reduce the import surplus by raising the price of imports relative to domestic goods and by decreasing purchasing power. In raising the domestic currency proceeds of export sales, a devaluation should move the producer up his marginal cost curve and lead to higher output. Such a procedure is a means of offsetting rising wages, but a cost-of-living allowance which keeps real wages constant tends, unless unemployment is allowed to rise, to defeat the devaluation. Anti-inflationary increases in sales and excise taxes pose a similar problem because they too lead to higher cost-of-living payments.

Since 1962 the government has pressed the position that wages should not rise more than productivity and that the growth rate of consumption must be restricted. In furtherance of this policy, it has applied pressure within Histadrut to moderate wage demands. The coalition government, dominated by Mapai, has also applied pressure on manufacturers to keep prices stable, agreeing, in return, not to raise taxes.[2] When wage drift and demand pressures nevertheless allowed incomes to rise appreciably, the government was caught in its agreement not to raise direct or indirect taxes. To a certain extent, raising indirect tax rates would be self-defeating, since their connection with the consumer price index and the cost-of-living allowance would enable labor to quickly recoup its reduced income. The cost-of-living allowance and the numerous agreements with both labor and employers have thus prevented the government from pursuing an effective tax policy to decrease domestic absorption.

Monetary Policy

The conduct of monetary policy is under the direction of the Bank of Israel. The Bank's control of money supply growth has been hampered by its inability to curtail the accumulation of large foreign-exchange holdings, which accounted for 60 percent of the increase in financial assets between 1960 and 1965. Moreover, the Bank must accommodate the government's deficit financing needs. In many periods government borrowing both from the Bank and from abroad has generated strong inflationary pressures which could not be fully offset by restrictions on private credit. Hence the Bank of Israel has placed primary emphasis on the distribution and allocation of credit.

17

Of the classical tools of monetary policy – open-market operations, rediscounting, and reserve requirements – the last has been the major instrument in Israel. The Bank of Israel has limited its use of rediscounting to export credits and before late 1966 did not use open-market operations. According to representatives of the Bank, it

> ...was unable to engage in open-market operations to any significant extent since its bond holdings had not yet been built up to an adequate level. Moreover, the Government believed that extensive sales of bonds by the Bank of Israel in a narrow market might impair the Government's ability to raise funds at regular intervals in order to sustain the development budget. [3]

In January 1964 reserve requirements were 69 percent on demand deposits and deposits in Israeli currency with terms up to 18 months. The Governor of the Bank of Israel was authorized, however, to exempt certain loans (which an individual bank might extend with the approval of the Bank of Israel) from the reserve requirements. [4] The limit for such "directed" credits was fixed at 22 percent of the total of deposits subject to reserve requirements. Thus, if the exemption from the reserve requirements were fully utilized, the 69 percent reserve ratio consisted of two elements: one representing 47 percent of the banks' liabilities, was required to be held in the form of liquid assets, and the other, an amount equal to 22 percent of the banks' liabilities, could be used for loans accorded priority by the Bank of Israel. (See Table 3.)

In addition to "directed" credits, credits from government deposits are also distributed by the Bank of Israel according to rules prescribed by the government. The purpose of the selective credit control is to ensure that "essential" enterprises – particularly those producing for export – are not adversely affected by credit restrictions. Controlled credit is extended at a lower rate of interest than that for ordinary bank credit.

Credit controlled by the Bank includes rediscounts, credits within the framework of the 22 percent exempted from reserve requirements, credits granted from 25 percent of the deposits in approved unlinked savings schemes, and some of the foreign currency credits granted by the banking system. In recent years credit directly controlled by the Bank of Israel through these devices represented about 50 percent of all bank credit granted to the private sector.

High reserve requirements and a ceiling on interest rates below market rates led to a market for credit outside traditional bank credit. Israeli commercial banks, acting as intermediaries between individuals with loanable funds and businessmen, guaranteed bills

Table 3. RESERVE REQUIREMENTS AND THE BANKS'
          BALANCE SHEETS WHEN LOANED TO CAPACITY

Balance Sheet, No Directed Credits

Assets			Liabilities	
Cash Reserve		IL 69	Deposits	IL 100
Earnings Assets				
Regular Credits	IL 31	31		
		IL 100		IL 100

Balance Sheet, Maximum Directed Credits

Assets			Liabilities	
Cash Reserve		IL 47	Deposits	IL 100
Earnings Assets				
Regular Credits	IL 31			
Directed Credits	22	53		
		IL 100		IL 100

Balance Sheet, Some Directed Credits

Assets			Liabilities	
Cash Reserve		IL 59	Deposits	IL 100
Earnings Assets				
Regular Credits	IL 31			
Directed Credits	10	41		
		IL 100		IL 100

Balance Sheet, Including Export Funds

Assets				Liabilities	
Cash Reserve			IL 47	Deposits	IL 100
Earnings Assets					
Regular Credits					
Export Credits	4				
Free Use	27	31			
Directed Credits					
Export Funds	4				
Other	18	22	53		
			IL 100		IL 100

and promissory notes in return for an average commission of about 4 percent. In 1964 and 1965, the total amount of promissory note credit was equal to 36 percent of outstanding bank credit (see Table 4). While the maximum interest rate banks could charge on regular loans was 11 percent, the cost of credit was between 15 and 22 percent in the bill brokerage market. To restrain the further expansion of the trade in guaranteed promissory notes, the Governor of the Bank of Israel was authorized in January 1965 to control the volume of guarantees given by banks on privately discounted promissory notes.

A large part of export financing is supplied through special funds and arrangements administered by the Bank of Israel. Through its rediscount facilities, the Bank provides 30 percent of the funds in the Special Fund for the Financing of Exporters' Imports, with the remaining 70 percent supplied by banks from credit originating abroad or from deposits of foreign residents. Since the Bank rediscounts promissory notes of exporters at a 2 percent rate of interest and the lending banks at 9 percent, the average interest rate payable within the framework of such arrangements is 6 percent.

Table 4.   BANK CREDIT

	Outstanding Loans and Bills Discounted		Bill Brokerage (Bills Outstanding)	
	IL Millions	Percent Change	IL Millions	Percent Change
1964	1,482	--	540	41
1965	1,939	30.8	696	28.9
1966	2,137	10.2	901	29.5
1967	2,851	33.4	869	-3.6
1968	3,554	24.7	666	-23.4
1969	4,339	22.1	709	6.5

SOURCE: Outstanding loans, end of year, from Bank of Israel, Annual Reports. Bill brokerage, annual average, from Central Bureau of Statistics, Monthly Bulletin of Statistics (Jerusalem), March 1970, p. 126.

20

Another fund provides credit for purchases of local raw materials as well as the financing of production processes and export consignments. The participants in this fund are the Ministry of Finance, the Ministry of Commerce and Industry, the Bank of Israel, and the commercial banks. The combined share of the government and the Bank of Israel for the financing of this fund totals 40 percent, and that of the commercial banks 60 percent. Half of the banks' quota must be furnished from their own resources, which are subject to reserve requirements, while the remainder may be supplied within the framework of credit not subject to reserve requirements. (See Table 3.) Interest on credit granted from this fund was reduced at the beginning of 1963 from 7.5 percent to 6 percent.

Finally, in addition to imposing high reserve requirements on commercial banks, the Bank of Israel has tried to control the expansion of the money supply by reducing the liquidity of the public's financial assets. The attractiveness of less liquid deposits has been increased by raising interest rates, by linking deposits to the cost of living, by linking them to the value of the dollar (Pazak accounts) or allowing them to be kept in foreign currency (Tamam accounts).

Deposits in foreign currency during the mid-1960's amounted to about two-thirds of less liquid deposits, their main source being private restitution payments from Germany. Tamam and Pazak accounts induce receivers of restitutions and other transfers from abroad to put their foreign currencies at the disposal of the monetary authorities and discourage them from converting their assets into more liquid forms by providing a hedge against possible future devaluation losses as well as earning power. Growth in such deposits has no monetary impact, since the banks must redeposit the full amount with the Bank of Israel. However, they can easily be converted into domestic means of payment. To a certain extent, these deposits are held as speculative balances, with movements into and out of them determined by expectations about possible devaluation.

Less liquid deposits in domestic currency comprise deposits under various savings schemes and time deposits. Savings plans offer various combinations of interest rates, linkages to the cost-of-living index, and tax concessions. The banks are required to invest 60 percent of their total savings deposits in government approved securities; a further 25 percent may be used for granting credits subject to Bank of Israel control and the remaining 15 percent may be used at discretion.

1. Nadav Halevi and Ruth Klinov-Malul, *The Economic Development of Israel* (New York: Frederick A. Praeger, 1968), pp. 185–6.

2. Tax rates are very high in Israel. Tax payments according to the 1971/72 budget were expected to equal 41 percent of GNP. (This includes income taxes, sales and excise taxes, Social Security taxes and compulsory loans.) After Sweden, Israel has the highest proportion of its GNP paid in taxes. Income tax rates are particularly high. A married wage earner with two children who earns $6,300 pays an average income tax rate of 32 percent.

3. Confidential source.

4. These were primarily loans to enterprises producing for export or for the replacement of essential imports and loans deserving high priority for development purposes.

PART II

Israeli Economic Policies in the 1960's

INTRODUCTION: POLICY GOALS
AND ACCOMPLISHMENTS

In 1960 Patinkin, reporting on the first decade of the Israeli economy, wrote that the "major failure of economic policy was not moving the economy closer to economic independence."[1] His prescription was to curtail growth in consumption and investment and to direct GNP growth toward import substitutes and exports. He noted that the preponderant role of the government in financing investment would facilitate carrying out these restrictive policies. "Indeed," he argued, "since the receipts of the development budget are likely to get the first impact of the drop-off of foreign aid, such a curtailment would come almost automatically."[2]

In 1964 a convergence of three events forced the acceptance of the restrictive policies Patinkin had prescribed. Knowing that German reparations payments were to end in 1966, the government also realized that Israel's long expected admittance to associate membership in the EEC might not occur because of politically motivated opposition from France,[3] and an exceptionally large jump in the 1964 current account deficit (28 percent) shocked the monetary and fiscal authorities. Faced with the loss of an important means of financing imports, the unexpected closing of an avenue to expanding exports, and a sharply higher deficit, the Israeli Government recognized that it had to halt the deterioration in the balance of trade caused by the economy's rapid growth. In its *Annual Report 1964*, the Bank of Israel pointed to slower economic growth as the means of improving the country's trade position.

> The large growth of the import surplus was due to a combination of factors: the rise in imports stemming from the intensification of general economic activity; mounting domestic demand, which caused imports of consumer goods and raw materials to expand faster than the national product and also had an adverse effect on exports; and the accumulation of stocks of imported raw materials.[4]

A recession was viewed by policymakers as a transitional state which would enable the economy to resume a more rapid growth path with exports as the leading sector. Nevertheless, the future growth rate was expected to be lower than that previously attained. While this reflected expectations of slower immigration and lower capital transfers, it was essential to the export-led growth model. In any economy which is approaching full employment, rising consumption tends to divert resources from exports to the domestic market, and this problem was particularly acute in Israel. Since large foreign-capital transfers to Israeli citizens (mainly German restitution payments) had enabled consumption to rise more rapidly than income from domestic resources, income from domestic activity would have to be more restrained than would be required without these large transfers. Economic growth also had to be slowed in order to counter the effects of the pervasive cost-of-living escalator clauses which, coupled with high domestic demand, had helped make Israel a high wage area and had tended to price Israeli goods out of foreign markets.

The Governor of the Bank of Israel, David Horowitz, called for a firm deflation policy along the lines of that then currently maintained by the British Labor Government. The pillars of such a policy would be stringent control over bank credit, a budget surplus, an incomes policy, a reduction in foreign borrowing, and further import liberalization.[5] The Chairman of the Board of Directors of the Bank Leumi, Israel's largest bank, seconded Horowitz's call for an anti-inflation policy.[6] In November 1965 the newly elected Government, in introducing its budget for the following fiscal year, declared the need for slower economic growth.[7] The immediate concern of the recession policy was to decrease imports, which could be expected to follow fairly automatically from slower economic growth but would not be maintained with renewed economic activity. The long-term goal was to shift resources into export industries by increasing the competitiveness of Israeli products and by making the export market relatively more attractive than the domestic market.

The success or failure of these policies cannot be judged simply by measuring whether the trade gap narrowed or widened. The Six-Day War and the subsequent period of hostilities pushed defense imports, which are included in imports of services, far above their pre-1967 level. Otherwise, imports and exports of services have usually been in near balance.[8] Hence commodity trade, where Israel's import surplus has always been very large, deserves primary attention. It must be noted, however, that Israel's two main commodity exports are relatively uninfluenced by domestic policies: citrus exports vary most directly with weather conditions, while diamond exports are to a large extent determined by the quotas set by an international cartel based in London. To judge the effects of discretionary policies on exports, these must be omitted from consideration. Finally, since

Israel's historical experience has tended toward narrowing, in percentage terms, the trade gap, continued gains in exports relative to imports might signal a continuation of these long-term trends rather than success of the recession policies. Therefore, deviations from the trend growth rates, i.e. whether exports grew more rapidly and imports less so than they had during previous years, is the most appropriate measure.

Bearing these qualifications in mind, several general conclusions can be drawn from the data available. First, variations in imports were the major factors in both the recovery in the trade balance during 1966–1967 and the new trade balance crisis in 1969. The sharp drop in imports during the recession accomplished an immediate narrowing of the trade gap, but, as expected, this temporary gain was not maintained during the subsequent period of rapid growth in 1968–1969. Secondly, the recession did have the long-term effect of raising the growth rate of industrial exports, exclusive of diamonds. Changes in basic orientation and profitability occurred, and exports of industrial goods from industries which had their primary market in Israel were significantly higher than would have been expected from previous trends. Finally, the November 1967 devaluation, higher export subsidies, and a domestic wage-price freeze continued to bolster the profitability of exports in the recovery period and largely offset the contractionary effects of rising home demand.

1.   Don Patinkin, *The Israel Economy: The First Decade* (Jerusalem: The Falk Project for Economic Research in Israel, November 1959), p. 132.
2.   *Ibid.*, p. 139.
3.   See Mordechai E. Kreinin, "Israel and the European Economic Community," *Quarterly Journal of Economics*, LXXXII (May, 1968) for a discussion of the effects of EEC trade policies on Israel's economic development.
4.   Bank of Israel, *Annual Report 1964*, p. 34.
5.   *The Jerusalem Post*, November 14, 1965, p. 2.
6.   *The Jerusalem Post*, November 15, 1965 and January 21, 1966.
7.   Budget Address of Finance Minister Sapir, *The Jerusalem Post*, November 19, 1965, p. 11.
8.   Exports of services are an increasingly important fraction of foreign trade due to the rapid growth of tourism. In 1968, they accounted for 47.1 percent of total exports on current account.

CHAPTER III

THE BOOM AND THE RECESSION

Restraining the Boom: 1964–1965

Monetary Policy

In 1964 the Bank of Israel took several steps to moderate the rapid growth of the money supply which had been fueled by massive foreign currency conversions. Reserve requirements on new demand deposits were raised from 69 percent to 89 percent from January to April, when most of the seasonal accumulation of foreign exchange reserves takes place (see Table 1). When the higher reserve requirements were lifted in May, the banks agreed to use all of the released reserves to buy government bonds; as a result, during the first half of 1964 the growth of the money supply slowed to under 5 percent, compared with 20 percent in the first half of 1963 (see Table 2). The Bank of Israel's efforts at restraint were aided by the sharp increase in the import surplus in 1964, which automatically slowed the rate of increase of foreign-exchange reserves.

To restrain bank credit expansion further, in April the government required the banks to loan it IL 50 million in fiscal year 1964/1965. Subscriptions to this loan were to be met by the transfer of half of any increase in bank deposits. Taking into account the reserve requirement of 69 percent, this left the banks with the equivalent of only 15.5 percent of any increase in deposits from which they could extend credit to enterprises that did not benefit from the "directed" credits.

As Table 3 shows, these policy moves and the larger import surplus slowed money supply growth in 1964 to 6 percent, less than the 10.4 percent rise in real GNP. Monetary growth in 1964 was substantially lower than in the previous two years, when it had averaged 29 percent, a rate two to three times faster than growth in real GNP.

In the first quarter of 1965 the formal reserve requirement remained at 69 percent, with 22 percent of reserves exempted. Of the exempted portion, 6 percent had to be allocated for financing exports and the remaining 16 percent for other types of controlled credit. Despite its concern over controlling the growth of the money

28

Table 1. SUMMARY OF MONETARY POLICY ACTIONS

	Reserve Requirements on Demand Deposits	Controlled Credit Exempt from Reserve Requirements	Reserve Requirements on Time Deposits (Over 6 Months)	Change in Rediscounts and Loans (IL Millions)	Open-Market Sales (IL Millions)
1963 IV	69%	22%	69%		
1964 I	89*	22	69		
II	69 (May)	22	69		
III	69	22	69		
IV	69	22	69	29.9**	
1965 I	69	22	69		
II	68 (June)	23 (June)	69		
III	68	23	69		
IV	68	23	69	23.6**	
1966 I	68	24 (Feb)	69		
II	68	24.5 (June)	69		
III	67 (Aug)	24.5	10 (Sept)		
IV	65 (Dec)	25 (Nov)	10	122.2**	-15.1 (IV)
1967 I	65	25	10		
II	65	25	10		

*On new deposits.   **Annual data.   SOURCE: Bank of Israel, Annual Reports.

29

Table 2. THE MONEY SUPPLY, QUARTERLY
(Seasonally Adjusted)

	IL Millions	Percent Change
1963 I	1359.5	8.5
II	1468.5	8.0
III	1524.3	3.8
IV	1602.1	5.1
1964 I	1673.7	4.5
II	1675.9	0.1
III	1675.4	-0.0
IV	1705.5	1.8
1965 I	1748.2	2.5
II	1796.7	2.8
III	1861.7	3.6
IV	1925.4	3.4
1966 I	1900.9	-0.1
II	1955.4	2.9
III	2005.4	2.6
IV	1990.2	-0.8
1967 I	2131.5	7.1
II	2309.5	8.4
III	2492.8	7.9
IV	2529.9	1.5
1968 I	2699.7	6.2
II	2792.7	3.4
III	2844.1	1.8
IV	2924.7	2.8
1969 I	3124.4	6.8
II	3013.4	-3.6
III	3004.7	-0.3
IV	3023.2	0.6

SOURCE: Central Bureau of Statistics, Monthly
Bulletin of Statistics (Jerusalem),
several issues. Data for 1963-1965
seasonally adjusted by the author.

Table 3.   THE MONEY SUPPLY

	Year-end Balance (IL Millions)	Percent Change During the Year
1963	1,609	28.1
1964	1,707	6.1
1965	1,899	11.2
1966	2,008	5.7
1967	2,539	26.4
1968	2,899	14.2
1969	2,970	2.5

SOURCE: Bank of Israel, Annual Reports 1965-1969.

supply, the Bank of Israel chose to lower reserve requirements in the second quarter by one percentage point and to raise exempted reserves to 23 percent for banks that would earmark 8 percent of their reserves for export financing. The reduction in liquidity requirements was thus aimed primarily at making additional credits available to the Export Fund. Previously some banks had left unused a part of the "directed" credits because they had to match them with equal credits from their "free" funds, which they preferred to use for more profitable transactions. The Israeli authorities expected the conditional reduction in the liquidity requirements to encourage the banks to fulfill their obligations to the Export Fund. To facilitate the extension of other types of controlled credit in this period of increasing monetary restraint, the quota for directed credits was raised another 1 percent, to 24 percent, between October 1965 and February 1966.

Because the banks were not regularly meeting their reserve requirements, the Bank of Israel in February 1965 raised the penalty rate for deficiencies from a fixed rate of 10 percent to a progressive rate varying from 10 to 20.5 percent. This change significantly reduced the extent to which liquidity ratios were not observed in 1965 and was thus one of the factors contributing to the decrease in the growth rate of credit.

The money supply in 1965 grew by 11 percent, only moderately faster than the growth of real GNP. From September to the end of the year, however, the money supply actually declined slightly, despite the fact that foreign-exchange reserves increased at a rising rate. An important reason for the slower growth of the money

31

supply was that, contrary to earlier experience, recipients of restitution payments preferred to deposit a larger share of their funds in foreign currency accounts. During 1965, when rumors of devaluation and the collapse of the speculative boom in the stock market and in real estate increased their attractiveness, such deposits rose by IL 170 million, to IL 862 million.

Bank of Israel restrictions on the total amount of bills which the banks were permitted to guarantee also slowed the growth rate of the bill brokerage market in 1965. The outstanding amount of bills at the end of 1965 was IL 696 million, an increase of 29 percent, compared with an increase of 41 percent in 1964 (see Table 4).

Table 4.   BANK CREDIT

	Outstanding Loans and Bills Discounted		Bill Brokerage (Bills Outstanding)	
	IL Millions	Percent Change	IL Millions	Percent Change
1964	1,482	--	540	41
1965	1,939	30.8	696	28.9
1966	2,137	10.2	901	29.5
1967	2,851	33.4	869	-3.6
1968	3,554	24.7	666	-23.4
1969	4,339	22.1	709	6.5

SOURCE: Outstanding loans, end of year, from Bank of Israel, Annual Reports. Bill brokerage, annual average, from Central Bureau of Statistics, op. cit., March 1970, p. 126.

Another factor was the increase in the effective interest rate paid by borrowers as a result of some banks raising their commission rates. Costs to borrowers in this market in 1965 ranged from 15 to 22 percent.

Fiscal Policy

In October 1964 the Minister of Finance announced a fiscal policy which called for the curtailment of government spending, increased tax collection, a halt in the construction of public buildings, a cut in consumer subsidies, and special measures to aid exporters. Furthermore, wage increases in 1965 (excluding payment of the cost-of-living allowance) were to be confined to 3 percent. These measures were designed to curb inflation and to reduce the import surplus.

The proposed 1965/66 budget called for expenditures of IL 3.7 billion, about 17 percent higher than in the proposed 1964/65 budget (see Table 5). The increase was substantially lower than the rise in budgetary expenditures, 23 and 28 percent, respectively, experienced in the preceding two years. The reduction reflected slower growth in development expenditures. Proposed allocations for housing, water projects, and mining development were actually lower than in the 1964/65 budget.

Except for a new tax on certain services, the budget proposal did not provide for a change in tax rates. Substantial increases in tax yields were expected, however, because of the increase in population, higher personal income, and more efficient tax collection. Despite the expected increase in tax revenues, foreign loans of almost IL 600 million would be needed to balance the budget.

This budget did not in fact result in a major absorption of liquidity in the economy. While the estimates for 1965/66 showed that the budget's withdrawal of income from the economy would exceed its purchases of goods and services by IL 255 million (or by IL 100 million more than in 1964/65), the restraining effect of this surplus was offset by the government's domestic credit operations. In 1965/66 the development budget exceeded the government's net borrowing from domestic sources by IL 596 million. Thus, the budget would add substantially to the purchasing power of the rest of the economy. In effect, large net domestic credit expansion was to be financed by borrowing abroad.

The elections scheduled for the fall of 1965 – both by the Histadrut and in the country as a whole – weakened the resistance of the leadership to unusually large wage demands. After protracted negotiations, an agreement signed in August 1964 called for a new scale of 20 grades for administrative personnel in the public service. The regrading of such personnel resulted in a 25 percent increase in salaries, made retroactive to April 1, 1964, despite the government's original budget plan to raise wages only 3 percent. After the wage increases had become effective for the administrative personnel, the professional civil servants asked for the restoration of the previous differential. Negotiations began in the summer of 1965, and in November an 18 percent increase, retroactive to April 1, 1964, was agreed upon. Although the payment of the arrears was to be spread over five instalments during the first part of 1966, at the beginning of 1966 some of the professionals renounced a part of their back pay, or agreed to receive it in bonds, in order to support the government's price and incomes policy of restraint.

Table 5. SUMMARY OF GOVERNMENT BUDGETS
(Millions of Israeli Pounds)

	1964/65 Proposal	1964/65 Actual	1965/66 Proposal	1965/66 Actual	1966/67 Proposal	1966/67 Actual	1967/68 Proposal	1967/68 Actual
Current Revenues	2407	2451	2920	2865	3544	2986	3756	3295
Grants and Loans	1058	1059	914	1216	910	1620	1218	2356
TOTAL	3465	3510	3834	4104	4454	4606	4974	5631
Ordinary Expenditure	2275	2302	2665	2625	3239	3157	3504	4022
Development Expenditure	855	799	1000	1135	885	1048	1233	1154
TOTAL	3130	3101	3665	3760	4124	4205	4737	5176
Balance on Current Account	-54	149	255	240	305	-171	252	-727
TOTAL DEFICIT	-723	-736	-579	-895	-420	-1219	-1218	-1881

SOURCE: Bank of Israel.

34

Toward the end of 1964 the government adopted a recommendation of the Committee of Inquiry into the Income Tax Structure to reduce the regular income tax rates in the higher income tax brackets. As a result, the net income of all upper income brackets, including non-civil servants, increased between 5 and 9 percent. Application of the new taxes was made retroactive to April 1, 1964, but the refunds were applied against taxes due in 1965.

Developments in the closing months of 1965/66 were not as favorable as the budget had anticipated. The government's activities had added IL 895 million to the purchasing power of the economy (see Table 5). An even larger deficit was avoided only by slowing down development budget outlays, although these still slightly exceeded the original budget estimate. Thus, while the official economic policy aimed at restraining effective domestic demand, the budget probably contributed little to this objective in 1965/66.

The Recession: 1966–1967

Fiscal Policy

The proposed budget for 1966/67 again emphasized the need to stabilize the economy in order to achieve the foreign trade objectives. To restrain the boom and over-employment which he believed still characterized the economy and to balance projected revenues and expenditures, the Minister of Finance proposed raising taxes and cutting the development budget by 14 percent. The ordinary budget surplus was projected at IL 305 million; to effect this, income tax rates in the upper income tax brackets were increased by 2–2.5 percent, and various indirect taxes were also to be raised. Credit granted through the development budget was to be reduced, and the net excess of expenditures and loans granted was to amount to IL 420 million, compared to IL 895 million for 1965/66. (See Table 5.)

The budget contained other proposals to reduce total demand and to facilitate a restructuring of production toward exports. As a restraining measure, the government planned more attractive savings plans as well as income tax deductions and other benefits for the purchases of life insurance. The restructuring of industry was to be aided by a reduction in tariffs to induce greater efficiency and better quality control in local industry as well as to curb price increases. In order to increase labor mobility into export industries, the government planned to seek the transferability of pension rights as well as aid in retraining and in obtaining new housing. Exports were to be stimulated directly through tax rebates and indirect subsidies.[1]

The budget was based on two projections for 1966: that investment in the private sector would increase by 1.5 percent, in spite of the cut in the development budget, and that real GNP would rise by 7.5 percent – almost the same as the 8 percent rise in 1965. Employment was expected to rise by only 2.5 percent, while the labor force was expected to grow by 3 percent; these changes would ease the overfull employment conditions which had prevailed for several years. No widespread increase in unemployment was anticipated.

During the first quarter of 1966 the economy continued to slow, and, beginning with the second quarter, real GNP began to decline. Consumer spending was sharply cut as a result of the spreading uncertainty and pessimism regarding future income as unemployment began to increase and business profits declined. Reduced restitution payments from West Germany – much of which had been spent on housing and consumer durables – further lowered demand. The higher indirect taxes introduced in the 1966/67 budget also reduced consumer purchases. Auto purchases in the second quarter fell about 50 percent, and purchases of most other consumer durables were also considerably lower. Construction and its allied industries (building materials, trucking, etc.), which had long played an inordinately large role in the economy, continued the decline begun in 1965.

While the number of jobs was decreasing, the expansion of the labor force continued, increasing unemployment. The rise in wage rates and the retroactive pay increases, which had been contracted in 1965 and in early 1966, plus wage increments to compensate for the rise in the cost-of-living index in the latter half of 1965, added to production costs. Reduced demand for products, coupled with higher wages, adversely affected the demand for labor and aggravated the unemployment situation.

During the early months of 1966 the Finance Minister began to exert pressure on Histadrut to forego payment of the cost-of-living allowance due on July 1. Although the pressures to retain this long-accepted protection of the workers' purchasing power were enormous, Histadrut agreed to waive the allowance for the first time, thus setting the stage for similar waivers subsequently. Responding to further government pressure, in September Histadrut agreed to increase the cost-of-living allowance by only half of any increase in the cost-of-living index during 1967 and 1968. It also agreed that wage increases to be negotiated in 1968 would be kept in line with the increase in productivity. In return, the government committed itself not to increase taxes.

In spite of the spreading unemployment, the Finance Minister continued to advocate the dismissal of redundant workers. In June 1966, he stated that "the economic situation is not as bad as people think."[2] Pressure was applied to reduce the size of the civil service and the staff of the Jewish Agency.[3] Although in September the government reaffirmed its commitment to a policy of economic restraint, the sharp rise in the unemployment rate from 3.5 percent in 1965 to 9 percent in the third quarter of 1966 forced it to take some steps to aid employment. Having rejected appeals from economists for a devaluation, it decided to stimulate aggregate demand by increasing export subsidies. To stem the emigration of professionals, the government increased special grants for retraining and research and offered aid in establishing and expanding the receipt of research contracts by Israeli firms and institutes from abroad.[4]

As late as September 1966 the government was not fully aware of the extent of the recession. Although the Ministry of Finance stated that real GNP in 1966 as a whole would be 6 to 7 percent above the level in 1965 – a slight revision of its February projection of 7.5 percent[5] – real GNP in 1966 was in fact only 1.5 percent above 1965 and actually declined in the final three quarters of the year. Because tax revenue fell with economic activity, 1966/67 actually ended with a deficit rather than the planned surplus.

The initial budget for 1967/68, presented at the end of December 1966, reaffirmed the policy of restraint in order to achieve the balance of trade goals but committed the government to reversing the rise in unemployment. As a counter-cyclical measure, capital expenditures were to be 40 percent higher than in the previous year's initial budget, although only 18 percent higher than actual spending (see Table 5). To revive the depressed construction industry, there would be a sharp increase in the building of hospitals, schools, and other public institutions, and relief work and public works projects were also to be expanded. Since the current account surplus would cover only a quarter of the budgeted capital expenditures, domestic and foreign borrowing were planned to rise substantially.

The budget was based on an economic forecast of a 5 percent increase in real GNP, a reversal in the downtrend in total investment, and a 15 percent rise in industrial investment, as compared with the 25 percent decline in 1966. The deficit in the balance of trade, which had been sharply reduced from $535 million in 1965 to $452 million in 1966, was expected to decline by an additional $30 million. Increased incentives to exporters were to be offered, and an overall increase of 13 percent was expected in exports, including a 20 percent rise in industrial exports (other than diamonds). Additional incentives offered to foreign investors were expected to reverse the declining trend of the previous two years. Foreign investments were expected to increase by 6 percent in 1967 and presumably more in later years.[6]

As the recession continued during the first months of 1967, the government announced in March an additional budget of IL 400 million designed to accelerate the public works program and relieve unemployment. Additional measures were introduced to increase demand, including low-cost loans for home improvement. Although the Minister of Commerce and Industry warned the public in January that the recession might last another two years or more,[7] the new Law for the Encouragement of Capital Investments, passed to provide even greater incentives to both local and foreign investors, seemed to stimulate a major increase in the number of proposed investment projects submitted to the Investment Center for approval.

But the Six-Day War became a crucial factor at this point. As Kanovsky points out:

> All other things being equal.... it would seem that the stronger anti-recessionary policy, evidenced in both fiscal and monetary policy, would have had an impact on the economy, possible by the latter half of 1967 or more likely during 1968. There is, however, that intangible element referred to as confidence, which though not quantifiable, has very measurable effects on the actions of consumers, producers and investors.... It is difficult to know at what point this turn-around might have taken place. We know, in retrospect, that it was the Six-Day War, and its direct and indirect effects, which sparked the change from pessimism to optimism.[8]

Monetary Policy

The monetary policy objective for 1966 was "to ensure that the rate of growth of money supply should not exceed that of the national product."[9] Between the last quarter of 1965 and the second quarter of 1966, the money supply increased by only 1.6 percent, compared with 5.3 percent in the corresponding period in 1965. During the 15-month period of slower economic growth from the last quarter of 1965 through the end of 1966, the money supply increased by only 3.4 percent (see Table 2). While net foreign asset accumulation declined in 1966, government indebtedness rose strongly, more than counteracting the loss in foreign reserves (see Table 6).

By June 1966 it began to appear that the recession had developed further than had been anticipated. To halt the economic decline, the Bank of Israel lowered reserve requirements on demand deposits from 68 percent in June to 67 percent in August. In November reserve requirements were again reduced, to 66 percent, and in December to 65 percent. In addition, reserve requirements on time deposits were cut from 67 percent in the summer of 1966 to 10 percent in September. Controlled credit exempted from reserve requirements was raised to 24.5 percent in June and then to 25

Table 6.   SOURCES OF GROWTH IN FINANCIAL ASSETS

Percent Change in Financial Assets Due to Changes in

	Growth in Financial Assets (IL Millions)	Accumulation of Foreign Currency Assets	Expansion of Credit to the Public*	Expansion of Credit to the Government	Other Factors, Including Open-Market Operations	Total
1964	254	16.5	58.3	37.4	-12.5	100.0
1965	394	55.6	34.5	14.0	-4.1	100.0
1966	408	-17.2	72.8	46.3	-2.0	100.0
1967	1,473	45.4	35.2	23.6	-4.1	100.0
1968	1,338	-12.9	44.1	72.8	-4.0	100.0
1969	983	-109.8	56.7	142.7	10.4	100.0

*Includes rediscounts and loans from the Bank of Israel.

SOURCE: Bank of Israel, Annual Reports.

percent in November. These changes reduced effective overall reserve requirements from 44 percent in the second quarter of 1966 to 42.5 percent in the third quarter and then to 40 percent in the final quarter of the year.

During 1966 the Bank of Israel began using open-market operations. Under a new arrangement initiated in October, sales of the short-term securities which had been a means of raising funds for the government were taken over by the Bank of Israel to be used as an open-market instrument. The policy of the Bank during 1966 and 1967 was to encourage sales of the loan to ensure its widespread use, although this in effect reduced the liquidity of the commercial banks. The impact of sales, however, was offset by other measures, notably purchases of other securities in the Tel Aviv stock exchange, and eventually the sales themselves were slowed down by successive reductions in the interest rates, by less favorable terms to the agents, and by quotas on weekly issues.

The money supply grew 15 percent from the third quarter of 1966 through the second quarter of 1967. The main source of growth was government deficit financing, reflected in the striking rise in credit advanced to the government from the Bank of Israel. The government borrowed from the Bank IL 702 million for implementing plans to stimulate economic activity, and its net indebtedness to the banking system (including the Bank of Israel) increased by some 70 percent in both 1966 and 1967.

The much larger supply of funds and the decline in demand for credit connected with the fall in investment and the generally low level of economic activity pushed interest rates down. In the bill brokerage market, rates fell by 3 to 4 percentage points. Interest rates on the government short-term loan fell by 2 percentage points. Rates on various deposits also declined. In the medium-term bond market, since the large volume of funds available was matched by the rising volume of government bonds offered, interest rates remained unchanged.

During 1967 the rising trend of bill brokerage business was reversed. This was partly because of the failure of three banks that dealt chiefly in unguaranteed bills, which largely disappeared during the course of 1967. Even the volume of guaranteed bills fell because most banks had reached the maximum permitted volume of guarantees. Banks began to divert investors to time deposits on which the liquidity requirements had been reduced and the rate of interest paid to depositors raised. This development partially offset the expansionary effect of the 34 percent increase in bank credit to the public in 1967.

The Trade Balance: 1965–1967

Imports

As Chart 1 shows, total imports slipped below trend in 1965, as economic activity first slowed and then fell rapidly during the recession. Slower economic activity and restrictive monetary policy which decreased the economy's liquidity and raised interest rates lowered the demand for raw materials for both current production and for inventory, while the demand for investment goods was also weakened. Declines in iron, steel, and wood imports were directly connected with the slump in construction activity.

Since investment is cyclically the most volatile economic sector, it is not surprising that imports of investment goods fell most sharply during the recession (see Chart 2). Among imported investment goods, those for building and industry accounted for the major share of the cutback.

Raw material imports slowed in 1965, while industrial production did not peak until early 1966. Imports fell initially because production needs were met by drawing down stocks. During the recession raw material imports for industry followed closely the declining trend of industrial production (see Chart 2). The structure of imports changed, however, with imports for the domestic market falling while imports of raw materials for exported products (especially uncut diamonds) rose.

Imports of consumer goods declined in early 1965 because a heavy tax was imposed on imported cars, and then fell rapidly from the first quarter of 1966 to mid-1967 as unemployment rose (see Chart 3). The 1962–1965 trend was much higher than that for either 1955–1963 or 1958–1963, because prior to 1962 there had been import quotas on many consumer goods.

Imports thus responded to the recession as expected by policy-makers. The slowdown policy cut the level of commodity imports, excluding ships and aircraft, from $208 million (seasonally adjusted) in the fourth quarter of 1965 to $185 million in the first quarter of 1967, a drop of 11.1 percent. Imports declined precipitously further in the second quarter, but the outbreak of war in June had by then become an added factor. Nevertheless, the import decline through the first quarter was the largest experienced over a comparable time period since the 1952–1953 recession.

Exports

Moderating economic activity may benefit export industries by easing pressures for higher wages and by making labor more readily available. For example, diamond exports rose more rapidly in 1966, partly because the industry was able to hire additional workers.

41

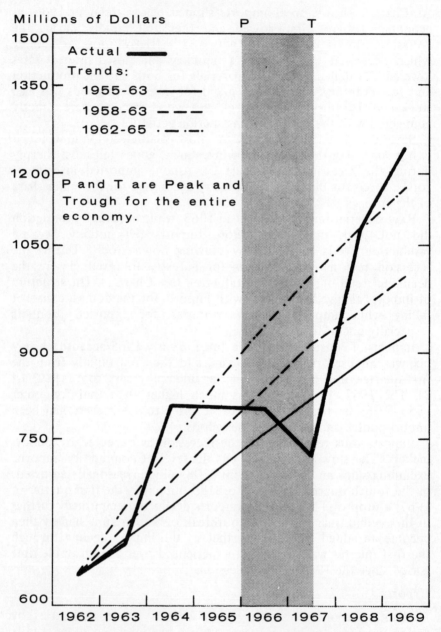

Chart 1
TOTAL COMMODITY IMPORTS

Millions of Dollars

P and T are Peak and Trough for the entire economy.

Actual ▬▬
Trends:
  1955-63 ——————
  1958-63 ― ― ―
  1962-65 ·―·―·

Source: Central Bureau of Statistics,
Monthly Foreign Trade Statistics.

Chart 2
IMPORTS AND INDUSTRIAL PRODUCTION

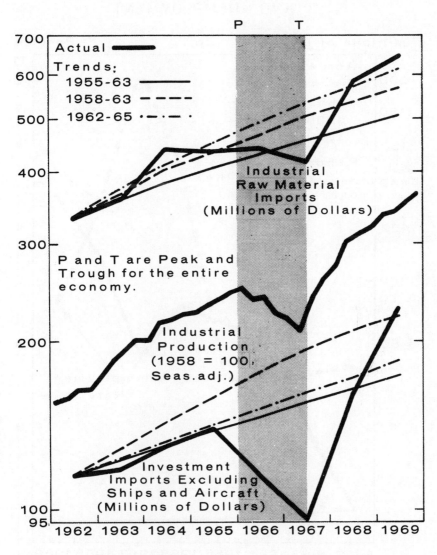

Source: Imports Data:
Central Bureau of Statistics,
Monthly Foreign Trade Statistics.

Production Data:
Central Bureau of Statistics,
Monthly Bulletin of Statistics.

43

Chart 3

CONSUMER GOODS IMPORTS AND UNEMPLOYMENT

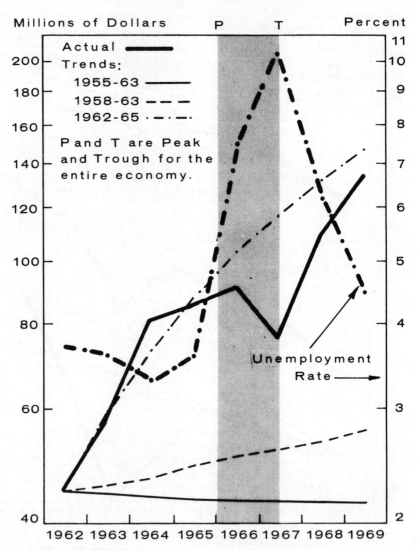

Millions of Dollars   P   T   Percent

Actual ▬▬▬▬
Trends:
1955-63 ————
1958-63 – – – –
1962-65 ·—·—·—

P and T are Peak and Trough for the entire economy.

Unemployment Rate →

1962 1963 1964 1965 1966 1967 1968 1969

Source: Imports Data:
Central Bureau of Statistics,
Monthly Foreign Trade Statistics.

Unemployment Rate :
Bank of Israel, Annual Reports.

44

During the boom year of 1964 employment in the industry had dropped 9 percent as employers were unable to hold on to workers bid away to higher wage areas. In 1965 employment was stable, while it gained 17.6 percent in 1966 and another 11.5 percent in 1967. (In contrast, total employment in the economy fell 0.3 percent in 1966 and 4.3 percent further in 1967.)

For most Israeli industries the domestic market is the major outlet, and it was expected that a decline in domestic demand caused by the recession would force them to turn to exports. In fact, it is clear that for virtually all industrial groups, exports made up a larger proportion of output in 1966 than in either of the previous two years (see Table 7). This trend was accentuated in 1967 when total output fell while exports continued to rise.

The most dramatic change occurred among minor industrial exports (listed as "other" in Table 7), where the quantity exported depended largely on the surplus remaining from the domestic market. In 1967 "other" industrial exports equaled 20 percent of total industrial exports. As Table 7 shows, only during the recession period did such industrial exports grow more rapidly than the production of these goods.[10] In 1965, at the peak of the boom, these exports had not expanded at all.

As Charts 4 and 5 show, exports from a broad group of industries oriented primarily to the domestic market have risen at an accelerated rate since 1965. This trend parallels that in Lovasy's study of inflation and exports, which showed that the effect of inflation was to prevent the diversification of exports and to depress the growth of minor exports.[11]

The small percentage of industries which actually increased their exports markedly during the recession[12] apparently included those whose current costs were in line with world prices. Such firms can more easily reallocate resources to export production following a drop in local demand that is not accompanied by an increased return on exports. This is probably the major reason why those industries whose exports expanded appreciably in 1967 also rose at above average rates in 1966, before higher export subsidies went into effect.

Industrial exports, excluding diamonds and minerals, did not rise even more rapidly in 1966 and 1967, because the export sector offered little profitability. In many areas where firms divide their output between markets, the domestic market in effect subsidizes exports, because domestic prices are usually higher than export prices.[13] Such firms sell their marginal output abroad or, because of moral pressure, export some minimum amount. Enterprises which receive tax advantages and loans from the development budget in particular must export a small amount to retain those benefits even if

Table 7. A COMPARISON OF INDUSTRIAL PRODUCTION AND INDUSTRIAL EXPORTS
(Percent Change in Volume over the Previous Year)

	Total Industry	Textiles and Clothing	Mining and Chemicals	Rubber and Plastics*	Food	Other
1964						
Production	14.0	15.9	17.9	20.4	13.3	13.2
Exports	9.1	22.7	27.8	-6.7	25.3	7.9
1965						
Production	10.0	16.8	21.1	11.1	6.2	8.7
Exports	9.0	3.1	23.8	2.0	4.9	0
1966						
Production	1.4	4.1	7.4	3.7	6.4	-3.6
Exports	11.8	10.8	10.4	6.0	6.3	23.2
1967						
Production	-3.1	-3.8	-0.6	-0.6	5.5	-5.4
Exports	9.5	20.0	54.7	-0.9	8.8	5.4

*Exports refer to tires, a principal component of rubber products.

SOURCE: Central Bureau of Statistics, op. cit.

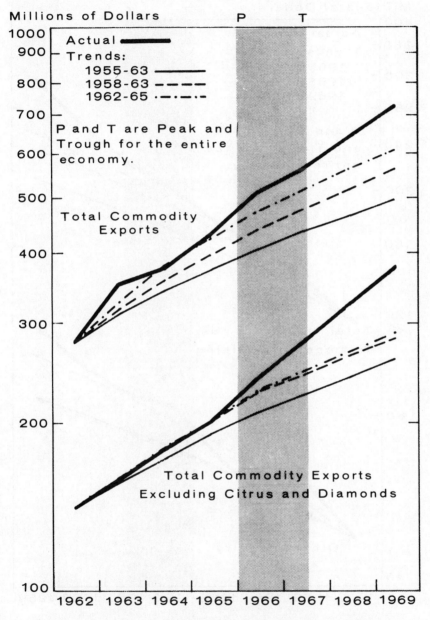

Chart 4

COMMODITY EXPORTS

Millions of Dollars

P   T

1000
900
800
700
600
500
400
300
200
100

Actual ▬▬▬
Trends:
1955-63 ——
1958-63 – – –
1962-65 ·–·–·

P and T are Peak and Trough for the entire economy.

Total Commodity Exports

Total Commodity Exports Excluding Citrus and Diamonds

1962 1963 1964 1965 1966 1967 1968 1969

Source: Central Bureau of Statistics, Monthly Foreign Trade Statistics

47

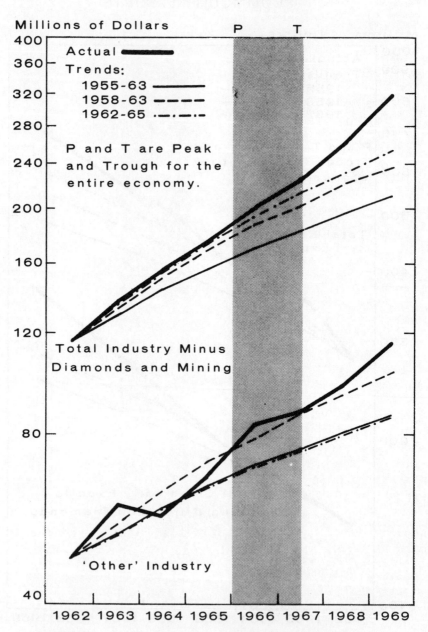

Chart 5
INDUSTRIAL EXPORTS

Millions of Dollars   P   T

Actual ▬▬▬
Trends:
    1955-63 ————
    1958-63 ————
    1962-65 —·—·—

P and T are Peak
and Trough for the
entire economy.

Total Industry Minus
Diamonds and Mining

'Other' Industry

Source: Central Bureau of Statistics,
Monthly Foreign Trade Statistics

they could sell their products more profitably in Israel. In some industries even variable costs exceed the return from exports, so that a decline in domestic demand in itself is insufficient to make exports profitable.

Although average variable costs fall sharply when capacity is unutilized[14] a move from domestic to export production may involve additional costs, such as the capital costs of redesigning or packaging to meet foreign tastes. In addition, there are the marketing costs of establishing new outlets. Thus, in practice, even with unused capacity, the average variable costs of exports may be appreciable.

In early 1966 the new national wage agreements that went into effect raised labor costs by 19 percent (including a 7 percent cost-of-living adjustment). While the recession eventually did affect wage demands, the strength of the labor movement and the coincidence that new contracts went into effect just as the recession began prevented wages from adjusting to the changed economic conditions as rapidly as they might have. Instead, there was a greater rise in unemployment and cutback in output.

Until late in 1966 the government resisted the demands of exporters for higher export premiums. As the unemployment rate jumped from 5.3 percent in the first half of 1966 to 9.4 percent in the second half, the government chose to stimulate exports by increasing export subsidies rather than through a devaluation. Since 1962 only a small number of industries received export subsidies – namely, the textile and clothing manufacturers and several agricultural enterprises, which needed to dispose of surpluses. In 1966 the government instituted a general system of incentives covering all export items. Enterprises were given tax rebates based on the percentage of output which they exported and their value added of the exports. These incentives, which were instituted in April 1966, were at first very small – only 0.5 percent to 3.5 percent of the value of exports. By November, however, they had been doubled.[15] Since low rates were in effect for most of the year, the incentives did not greatly influence the level of exports during 1966. However, the much larger export premiums granted textiles and clothing at the beginning of 1966 had a strong effect in 1966, although the contraction of the domestic market was also important. The volume of textile and clothing exports rose 11 percent in 1966 after increasing by only 3 percent in 1965.

During the 18-month recession the most noticeable effect of slower economic growth on exports was the marked rise in minor industrial exports.[16] Israel had clearly been hampered by the inflationary effect noted by Lovasy: inflation had inhibited the diversification of exports.

1. *Jerusalem Post*, March 4, 1966, p. 3.
2. *The Jerusalem Post*, June 17, 1966, p. 1.
3. *The Jerusalem Post*, July 29, 1966, p. 3.
4. Eliyahu Kanovsky, *The Economic Impact of the Six-Day War* (New York: Frederick A. Praeger, Inc., 1970), p. 33.
5. *Ibid.*
6. *Ibid.*, pp. 34−35.
7. *The Jerusalem Post*, May 14, 1967, p. 4.
8. Kanovsky, *op cit.*, p. 39.
9. Confidential source.
10. Exports of armaments are included in "other" industrial exports. While arms exports rose significantly in the post-1967 period, they did not affect the shift noted here.
11. Gertrude Lovasy; "Inflation and Exports in Primary Producing Countries," *International Monetary Fund Staff Papers*, March 1962.
12. Bank of Israel, *Annual Report 1968*, p. 57.
13. Bank of Israel, *Annual Report 1966*, p. 59.
14. In Israel, it is so difficult to fire workers that labor costs are very much like fixed costs.
15. Bank of Israel, *Annual Report 1966*, p. 56.
16. In Chapters V and VI, we examine from which sectors the additional domestic resources flowing into these exports came and the establishment of new export industries.

CHAPTER IV

THE ECONOMIC UPTURN: 1967–1969

Monetary Policy

The revival of economic activity since mid-1967 and the simultaneous large increase in budget deficits were accompanied by a rapid monetary expansion. As Table 1 shows, the money supply rose by 26 percent in 1967, compared to only 6 percent in 1966. The main forces responsible for this expansion were a large accumulation of foreign currency assets and a strong upsurge in bank loans. As Table 2 shows, the higher demand for bank credit came from the government as well as from the public, although in the latter case it constituted in part a shift from the bill brokerage market to regular bank loans.

During the second half of 1967 the recovery in economic activity was so rapid that some reassessment of monetary policy became necessary. Consequently, the monetary authorities, while not returning to a policy of credit stringency, no longer felt it was necessary to add actively to liquidity. Monetary growth slowed despite the rise in economic activity, as the Bank of Israel increased its open market sales of the short-term loan by IL 108 million (see Table 3). After the Six-Day War the net foreign currency assets of the banking system shot up by $110 million as money from world

Table 1.   THE MONEY SUPPLY

	Year-end Balance (IL Millions)	Percent Change During the Year
1966	2,008	5.7
1967	2,539	26.4
1968	2,899	14.2
1969	2,970	2.5

SOURCE: Bank of Israel, Annual Reports 1967–1969.

51

Table 2.

SOURCES OF GROWTH IN FINANCIAL ASSETS

	Growth in Financial Assets (IL Millions)	Percent Change in Financial Assets Due to Changes in			
		Accumulation of Foreign Currency Assets	Expansion of Credit to the Public*	Expansion of Credit to the Government	Other Factors, Including Open-Market Operations	Total
1967	1,473	45.4	35.2	23.6	-4.2	100.0
1968	1,338	-13.0	44.0	72.8	-3.8	100.0
1969	983	-109.8	80.6	142.8	10.4	100.0

*Includes rediscounts and loans from the Bank of Israel.

SOURCE: Bank of Israel, Annual Reports.

Table 3.   SUMMARY OF MONETARY POLICY ACTIONS

	Reserve Requirements on Demand Deposits	Controlled Credit Exempt from Reserve Requirements	Reserve Requirements on Time Deposits (Over 6 Months)	Rediscounts and Loans (IL Millions)	Open-Market Operations** (IL Millions)
1967 III	65%	25%	10%		-108 (III)
IV	65	25	10	147.2*	
1968 I	65	25	10		-18
II	65 (May)	25	10 (May)		-102 (Aug)
III	70 (Sept)	25	15 (Sept)		
IV	70	25	15	41.5*	+11 (IV)
1969 I	70	25	15		+20 (I)
II	70	25	15		-47 (Apr)
III	70	25	15		+82 (Aug)
IV	70	25	15	371.6*	-35 (Nov)

*Annual data.

**Minus (-) indicates sales; Plus (+) indicates purchases.

SOURCE: Bank of Israel, Annual Reports.

53

Jewry flowed to Israel. A large proportion of these receipts was deposited with the Bank of Israel in a special Jewish Agency account, however, and was not converted into means of payment.

During 1968 the rate of economic expansion slowed considerably. The increase in money supply slowed to 14 percent as the rise in foreign currency assets became less pronounced because of the growth in the import surplus. In the second half of the year foreign currency reserves began to fall. Bank credits, on the other hand, continued their rapid expansion, since demand for new loans remained strong both from the government and private sectors. (See Table 2.)

As economic activity expanded in 1968 and the economy approached full employment, the monetary authorities became increasingly concerned about the rising liquidity which was continuously being fed by large budget deficits and strong credit demand from the public. In May 1968 the Bank of Israel raised reserve requirements on demand deposits from 65 percent to 70 percent and those on time deposits from 10 percent to 15 percent in an attempt to moderate the rapid increases in the money supply. The rise was to take place at the rate of 1 percent a month over a five-month period.[1] In addition, the Bank reduced its rediscounts and loans. From May to August it absorbed IL 102 million in excess liquidity through open-market operations.[2] (See Table 3.) The disappearance of the banks' free reserves in September[3] indicates that the Bank's tight money policy was beginning to restrain credit expansion to the private sector. As a result of these measures and the decline in foreign currency reserves, the rate of monetary growth slowed in the second half of 1968.

Despite substantial increases in credit to the public and private sectors, the money supply rose by only 2.5 percent in 1969. This was due in part to the sharp decline in net foreign assets as the import surplus rose (see Table 2) and in part to a shift toward less liquid deposits.

The tightness in the money market which began to be felt in the last quarter of 1968 and continued through 1969 was reflected by a rise in market interest rates, the incurring of large liquidity deficiencies by banks, and the revived growth of the bill brokerage trade.[4] A shortage of liquid assets prevented the banks from fully satisfying the relatively heavy demand for credit and checked the rate of monetary expansion. The chief cause of this scarcity was the external drain resulting from the sharp $280 million fall in the Bank of Israel's holding of gold and foreign exchange. (At the end of 1969 the gold and foreign currency reserves of the Bank of Israel stood at $382 million, equivalent to about two months of imports of goods and services at the 1969 rate of importing.) This factor, together with the growth of foreign currency deposits of Israeli residents as expectations of a devaluation grew, offset the expansionary influence of the deficit financing of the government budget.

Bank of Israel policy was designed to ensure the continuation of a tight money situation and thereby restrain the growth of domestic demand. Owing to the decline in the liquid assets of the banking institutions and the stability of the money supply, the central bank did not have to resort to further absorptive measures. Its policy during the year was largely of a regulatory nature, designed to prevent crises.[5]

To keep money from becoming too tight, the Bank decided to increase liquidity during the months of August through November through rediscounts and loans to the public (IL 327 million) and open-market operations (IL 24 million).[6] Nevertheless, liquidity ratios were maintained unchanged throughout 1969, and pressure was exerted on the banks to limit their import financing. In November the Bank announced that bank credits earmarked for financing imports would be reduced by half, but full credit would continue to be given on imports for export industries.

Fiscal Policy

The Budget and Defense Spending

In fiscal 1967/68, current expenditure soared while tax revenues lagged far behind, resulting in a large current account deficit, rather than the originally planned surplus (see Table 4). Since the government had greatly underestimated the size of the postwar defense budget[7], in June 1967 it announced a supplementary budget of IL 350 million for defense, which was to be financed by a 10 percent income tax surcharge (IL 100 million) and by a special defense loan (IL 250 million). A second supplementary budget of IL 522 million was proposed in September, IL 50 million for defense and the rest for civilian projects. This expenditure was to be fully financed by borrowing, IL 330 million from abroad and the remainder by an advance from the Bank of Israel of IL 142 million and by expected additional sales of IL 50 million of defense loan bonds.

Total budget expenditures in 1967/68 rose by 23 percent. Ordinary expenditures were up 27 percent, the most important factor being a 60 percent increase in defense outlays. Since current revenue rose by only 10 percent, the overall deficit increased 54 percent, to a record level of IL 1.9 billion. Of this, IL 651 million was financed from foreign sources. In April 1968 the government requested approval of another supplementary defense budget of IL

Table 4.

SUMMARY OF GOVERNMENT BUDGETS
(Millions of Israeli Pounds)

	1966/67 Actual	1967/68 Proposal	1967/68 Actual	1968/69 Proposal	1968/69 Actual	1969/70 Proposal	1969/70 Actual
Current Revenues	2986	3756	3295	3788	4186	4850	4850
Grants and Loans	1620	1218	2356	1826	2023	2462	2628
TOTAL	4606	4974	5631	5614	6209	7402	7478
Ordinary Expenditure	3157	3504	4022	4117	4791	6202	6278
Development Expenditure	1048	1233	1154	1263	1418	1200	1200
TOTAL	4205	4737	5176	5380	6209	7402	7478
Balance on Current Account	-171	252	-727	-329	-605	-1352	-1428
TOTAL DEFICIT	-1219	-1218	-1881	-1592	-2023	-2552	-2628

SOURCE: Bank of Israel, Annual Reports.

56

500 million. Of the needed funds, IL 300 million were to come from a public subscription to a new series of defense bonds and the remainder from a cut in the development budget.[8]

The war and continuing hostilities sharply raised defense expenditures. The defense budget for 1968/69 was initially planned as IL 2.2 billion, equal to 18 percent of GNP (which compares with 9 percent in the United States and about 4.5 percent in the Western European countries).[9] The defense budget for 1969/70 was officially given as IL 2.9 million, an amount two and a half times the size of the prewar budget.[10] In June 1969 the Minister of Finance reported that military expenditures had risen to an annual rate of IL 3.3 million, which would put military outlays on a par with gross investment in the economy and would be equivalent to 20.7 percent of GNP or 17.5 percent of total resources.[11] (These figures do not include the additional costs of civil administration in the occupied territories.)

The much higher level of military expenditures within the country (i.e. excluding arms purchases abroad) helped spark the economic upswing. About half of the defense budget was spent within Israel.[12] In addition to the much higher level of production in the military industries, the Defense Ministry stepped up its orders to other local industries for such items as processed foods, clothing, pharmaceuticals, electronic equipment, and vehicles. The much higher level of defense purchases abroad was an important factor in the sharp deterioration in the trade balance.

Export Promotion

Following the British devaluation in November 1967, the Israeli pound was devalued by 16.67 percent. During the months immediately following the Six-Day War the economy still had considerable slack, so there was no absorption problem, and the government was in such an unusually strong political position that it could assert unusual pressures on Histadrut and avoid the wage increases which would normally result from a devaluation. In this situation the devaluation could accelerate the growth in exports, make imports more expensive, and thus contribute to the solution of the balance of payments problem. From a cost standpoint, it was particularly important that the impact of the devaluation on the domestic price level be kept at a minimum, and to help minimize the effect of higher import prices, tariffs were reduced so that the level of customs duties in domestic currency were broadly left unchanged.

In addition to this orthodox method of stimulating exports, the government tried to promote export growth by organizing a number of economic conferences to bring together Israeli and foreign Jewish businessmen. One of these organizations, Volunteers for Israel

Products, consisted of Jewish businessmen in western countries who decided to provide direct contact for their Israeli counterparts and aid them in selling their products abroad. Another organization, known as American Trade and Industrial Development with Israel, Inc., was set up after the war and included many top executives of large department stores and retail chains. Members seek potential markets for Israeli products and also direct the Israeli producer in adapting himself to the more exacting demands of the American buyer. Since such efforts take time, they had not produced statistically significant effects on exports by 1969.

The most important economic conferences were held in Jerusalem in August 1967 and in April 1968. Following the war, the government decided to channel Jewish support for Israel towards private investment and increased trade. Sixty wealthy Jewish businessmen from 13 countries met in closed session with government leaders in August 1967. At the April conference over 500 businessmen from abroad met with a similar number of Israelis, including business, Histadrut, and government leaders. Kanovsky reports:

> The results of this conference were two-fold. On the level of concrete achievements there was a series of commitments to undertake specific investment projects, know-how and marketing agreements, and the expansion of certain firms. The American group, almost half of the foreign participants, came with 32 projects ready for implementation and another 25 in the formative state.... Agreements were made to provide local industrialists with know-how and marketing facilities, and commitments were given by retailing firms to increase purchases in Israel. The conference decided to set up an investment company capitalized at $100 million to invest in Israeli firms with a good record of earnings, as well as in new ventures....
>
> The direct contacts between Israeli and foreign businessmen provided a stimulus for improvements in the management of Israeli enterprises.[13]

It is difficult to determine what share of the postwar increase in exports, production, investment and the favorable economic climate was due to the economic conference and to the other organizations of foreign businessmen aiding Israel. But a statement by the outgoing president of the Israeli Manufacturers' Association in June 1969 is noteworthy:

> ...there is a tremendous confidence of business in the future of this country and its economy that goes beyond the rational. I think it's a direct outcome of the general sense of confidence resulting from

the Six-Day War. But as far as business and industry is [sic] concerned, it's all due to the Jerusalem Economic Conference. It brought us into direct contact with the really big buyers, and I do not mean to dismiss the significance of the investors. From there on, our industrialists were infused with a greater faith in the future of exports.[14]

Incomes Policy

During the immediate postwar period the government was also able to capitalize on its strengthened political position and the widespread feelings of national unity to persuade Histadrut to adopt far-reaching changes in its wage policy. Basic wage rates were to be frozen until the end of 1969. Cost-of-living bonuses would be paid once instead of twice a year, and only if the cost-of-living index had risen by at least 3 percent. Since there were no payments in either 1968 or 1969, this new policy was of importance in maintaining wage and price stability during the economic expansion.

Renewed Attempts at Budgetary Restraint: 1968–1969

The 1968/69 budget was designed to have a "neutral" effect on overall demand, since strong autonomous expansionary forces were foreseen. The overall deficit was to decline by 15 percent. A substantial amount of the budget was again to be financed from foreign sources, but domestic borrowing from the banking system was also to be substantial. Ordinary expenditure was to grow only slightly, with rising defense expenditures being offset by lower expenditures for social services. (The actual level of social services would not be reduced, however, since their financing was to be taken over by the Jewish Agency, whose activities are financed by foreign grants.) Capital expenditures were to be held steady. (See Table 4.)

The deficit on current account showed a modest decline in 1968/69 because of a rise in tax revenues, reflecting the recovery in economic activity. The overall deficit, however, rose 7.5 percent because of an expansion in defense and capital outlays. Despite the expansionary effect of the public sector's operations on the level of aggregate domestic demand, the surplus of domestic expenditure over domestic revenue actually contracted. The budget deficit was due entirely to larger outlays abroad and was therefore reflected primarily in the balance-of-payments deficit on current account, while its stimulative effect on domestic demand diminished.

The original budget for fiscal 1969/70 foresaw a rise of 29 percent over the previous budget in current expenditures – mainly because of higher expenditures for defense, education, and interest payments

59

on debt – but a 15 percent decline in capital outlays. Ordinary revenue was estimated to rise by 16 percent, solely as a result of economic expansion. But in May 1969 the government raised sales taxes on automobiles, television sets, some other consumer durables, and travel abroad in order to curb the rise in consumption. Even with these increases, however, the domestic borrowing requirements of the Treasury were much higher than in 1968/69, with most of the borrowing from the Bank of Israel.

The budget deficit in 1969, as in 1968, mainly contributed to the deterioration of the balance of payments. The 1969 deficit again resulted almost entirely from the increase in direct purchases abroad, whereas the surplus of domestic expenditure over income from domestic sources declined.[15]

The few measures undertaken by the authorities in 1969 to reduce private consumption were relatively mild and not very effective because the impending elections in the fall of 1969 acted as a deterrent to more effective measures.

The May 1969 rise in sales taxes and the sale of additional defense bonds represented the government's major fiscal moves, but many Israeli economists argued that these selective tax increases were far too small and would do little to restrain the overall rise in private consumption.[16] The government's ability to restrain consumption was severely hampered by the government's agreement, in return for Histadrut's accepting a wage freeze, not to increase taxes. Moreover, imposing a higher broad-based sales tax would add to the pressures on prices, thereby triggering demands for compensating cost-of-living payments.

Another step undertaken to reduce private consumption was the floating of a new series of defense bonds to be sold to the Israeli public. The campaign for the sale of these bonds was begun in early 1969, shortly after the announcement of the purchase of the Phantom jets from the United States, and the goal was to raise $100 million, about one-third of the cost of the planes. Although the government had promised Histadrut that the purchase of these bonds would not be officially compulsory, considerable pressures were in fact exerted, and the large majority of workers purchased the suggested quota of bonds.[17]

The Trade Balance: 1967–1969

Imports

Imports mounted in the second half of 1967 as the economic recovery began. While government officials had expected higher imports, they were surprised by the steepness of the rise. Initially economists at the Bank of Israel explained it as a temporary

phenomenon resulting from a rebuilding of depleted inventories.[18]
But when commodity imports reached new highs in 1969, after
soaring 43 percent in 1968, they once again became concerned over
the country's balance of trade. Instead of covering 73 percent of
commodity imports, as they had in 1967, exports covered only 60
percent in 1969. Moreover, the historical relationship between the
growth rate of imports and exports had been reversed: in 1968 and
1969 imports grew faster than exports.

Part of the rapid growth in imports was certainly due to inventory
accumulation. Inventories had fallen by IL 65 million in 1967 but
rose by IL 175 million in 1968, and a portion of this increase was
imported goods. An even more important factor, however, was the
heavy dependence of Israeli production on imports. Thus the rapid
growth in industrial production and the revival of investment outlays
necessarily led to large import requirements. Comparison of the
industrial production index with imports of raw materials reveals
that they were growing at very similar rates from mid-1967 through
1969 (see Chart 1).

Despite the resurgence of imports, the government continued the
import liberalization program. Tariff reductions of between 10 and
30 percent were announced for a wide range of industrial commodities in October 1968 and January 1969. In line with this policy
of exposing local industry to foreign competition, the Ministry of
Commerce and Industry in May 1969 approved a five-year plan to
reduce tariffs until the effective exchange rate for imports stood at
IL 5.50 per dollar of value added. This plan could reduce average
duties to under 30 percent by January 1, 1975.[19]

Exports

The recession appears to have achieved at least moderate success in
its ultimate goal: a shifting of production and investment into export
industries. As Charts 2 and 3 show, industrial exports (excluding
diamonds and minerals) rose considerably faster than their trend
growth rate through 1969. The diversion of production into exports
is further revealed by the growing proportion of exports in GNP,
from 19 percent in 1965 to 22 percent in 1967 and to 26 percent in
1969.

Table 5 compares the actual growth in imports, exports, and the
import surplus from the fourth quarter of 1965 through the end of
1969 with the levels projected as if previous trends had simply
continued during this period. The 1967 import surplus would have
been almost twice as large as it actually was if the 1962–1965 boom
or the 1955–1963 growth had gone on. Moreover, if the trends set in
motion during the recession had continued through 1969, commodity exports would have covered commodity imports[20], largely

61

Chart 1

IMPORTS AND INDUSTRIAL PRODUCTION

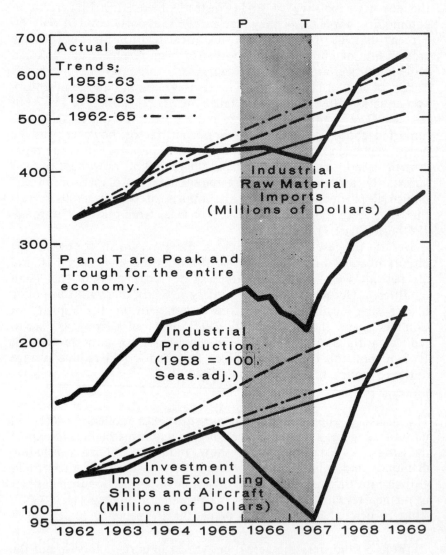

Source: Imports Data:
Central Bureau of Statistics,
Monthly Foreign Trade Statistics.

Production Data:
Central Bureau of Statistics,
Monthly Bulletin of Statistics.

Chart 2

COMMODITY EXPORTS

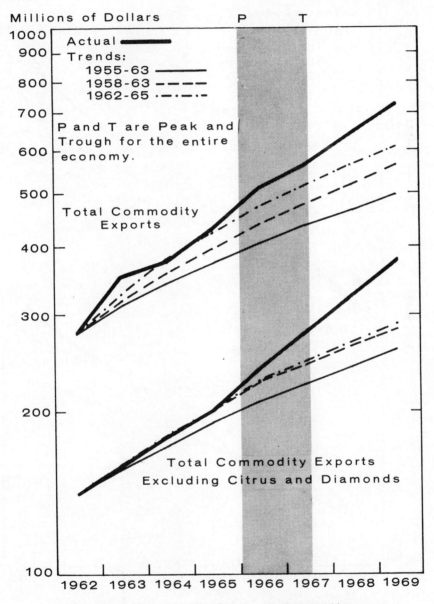

Millions of Dollars

P and T are Peak and Trough for the entire economy.

Actual ▬▬
Trends:
1955-63 ────
1958-63 ----
1962-65 -·-·-·

Total Commodity Exports

Total Commodity Exports Excluding Citrus and Diamonds

1962 1963 1964 1965 1966 1967 1968 1969

Source: Central Bureau of Statistics, Monthly Foreign Trade Statistics

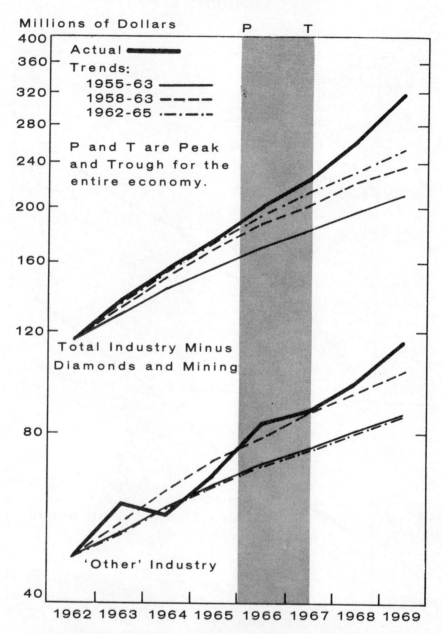

Chart 3
INDUSTRIAL EXPORTS

Millions of Dollars

Actual
Trends:
1955-63
1958-63
1962-65

P and T are Peak
and Trough for the
entire economy.

Total Industry Minus
Diamonds and Mining

'Other' Industry

Source: Central Bureau of Statistics,
Monthly Foreign Trade Statistics

Table 5.   EXPECTED VALUES OF COMMODITY IMPORTS,
            EXPORTS, AND THE COMMODITY TRADE
            SURPLUS COMPARED TO ACTUAL VALUES
                  (Millions of Dollars)

	1965	1966	1967	1968	1969
Imports (Net)					
Actual	$811	$814	$754	$1088	$1291
Trend 1962–1965	811	888	966	1043	1121
Trend 1958–1963	811	867	923	978	1034
Recession Rates	811	787	763	740	718
Exports (Net)					
Actual	406	477	517	602	683
Trend 1962–1965	406	453	500	547	594
Trend 1958–1963	406	446	485	524	564
Recession Rates	406	468	539	621	715
Import Surplus					
Actual	405	337	237	485	608
Trend 1962–1965	405	435	466	496	527
Trend 1958–1963	405	421	438	454	471
Recession Rates	405	319	224	119	3

Note: Exports and Imports were regressed against
        time to determine trends. The resulting
        equations are:

        Imports 1958-1963 = 180.0 + 55.8 time
        Imports 1962-1965 = 10.8 + 77.4 time
        Exports 1958-1963 = -21.1 + 39.4 time
        Exports 1962-1965 = -89.1 + 47.0 time

The recession trend assumes that the average
growth rate during 1966-1967 had prevailed.
Imports declined at a 3 percent annual rate
and exports rose at a 15.2 percent rate

SOURCE: Actual data from Central Bureau of Statis-
        tics, Monthly Foreign Trade Statistics,
        April 1970, Table I, p. 29.

because of the considerably lower level of imports. Although this did not happen, the table does indicate that it was imperative that Israel break the 1962–1965 pattern.

The recession did in fact lead to an appreciable expansion of exports, as Table 5 shows. In 1969 exports were between 15 percent and 21 percent higher than they would have been if previous trends had continued. It was the unexpected increase in imports which created the vast deterioration in the commodity trade account in 1969, though, of course, the higher exports were to a certain extent made possible only by the higher imports of raw materials and investment goods.

Credit for expanding exports in 1968 and 1969 must be shared by devaluation, higher subsidies, and the recession. Estimating the relative contributions of these three policy measures in creating more competitively priced exports, the Bank of Israel found that the wage and price stability caused by the restrictive monetary and fiscal policies increased Israel's competitive position vis-à-vis its major trading partners by about 8 percent. Devaluation increased the price advantage of Israeli exports by 14 percent, while the subsidies gave another 8 percent price gain. Thus by 1968 exporters had increased their price advantage by 30 percent.

In November 1967 the Israeli government followed the British devaluation by lowering Israeli currency from IL 3.00 = $1.00 to IL 3.50 = $1, a 16.67 percent reduction. The effects of this devaluation were not dissipated by higher prices because the economy was operating below full employment. In addition, the elan created by the Six-Day War made it possible for the government to successfully enforce a wage-price freeze during 1968.[21] The beneficial effects of this move must in large part be attributed to the employment situation of the economy, since the 1962 experience clearly showed that a devaluation at full employment would not have the desired results[22], especially when large foreign currency holdings in the hands of the Israeli public produce a "real balance effect" and wages are tied to the cost of living.

A second factor was the higher level of export subsidies, which by mid-1967 had risen to between 8 and 15 percent of value added.[23] Although this was not an insignificant level, only because the economy was not operating at full employment in 1968 and 1969 did the export subsidies fail to produce the strong price and income effects which would have diverted export goods back to the home market, as econometric models suggested they would. Simulations done by Subotnik confirmed Evans' conclusions, cited in Chapter 1: subsidies on exports had a detrimental effect on the balance of payments because of the strong income effect.[24] Thus the effect of the subsidies cannot really be separated from the fact that the

Table 6.   MEASURES OF ECONOMIC DEPENDENCE[a]

	Import Surplus as a Percent of Domestic Resources[b]	Exports as a Percent of Imports (Goods and Services)
1955	18.7	33.7
1956	19.8	33.3
1957	16.4	39.8
1958	14.1	41.3
1959	11.6	47.6
1960	11.1	52.7
1961	12.1	49.6
1962	16.5	51.4
1963	13.2	59.4
1964	14.8	54.7
1965	11.6	59.2
1966	9.0	67.4
1967	10.4 (9.3)[c]	65.5 (68.2)[c]
1968	13.6 (12.5)[c]	63.2 (65.4)[c]
1969	14.5 (13.3)[c]	60.4 (62.7)[c]

[a]The ratios were computed from data in current prices.

[b]GNP plus the import surplus.

[c]Assumes that Government service imports, mainly defense, remained at the 1966 level.

unemployment rate still averaged 6 percent in 1968. Although the unemployment rate averaged 4.5 percent in 1969, this was still a full percentage point higher than the rate had been in the years 1961–1965.

Although exports grew only 15 percent in 1969 after rising 22 percent in 1968, the more sluggish increase in commodity exports resulted mainly from the smaller gain posted by diamonds and the leveling off of the growth rate for citrus — branches which accounted for 45 percent of all exports. Industrial exports from branches directly affected by domestic demand conditions rose 18.5 percent in 1969, after climbing 29 percent in 1968, but even the slower 1969 growth was far higher than in 1964 and 1965, when it averaged only 9 percent.[25] "Other" industrial products again recorded a 15 percent rise in 1969, as they had in 1968.[26] As a proportion of GNP, exports rose from 19 percent in 1965 to 26 percent in 1969; later chapters will examine the shifting of real resources which made this export growth possible.

The slowdown policy was aimed at increasing the economic independence of Israel, a factor which is usually measured by the ratio of the import surplus to domestic resources or by the proportion of imports covered by exports. And the recession period proved that economic dependency is not an inherently necessary part of the Israeli experience, as some have stated.[27] As Table 6 shows, there was slow but steady progress from 1955 to 1963. During the recession, in a sharp break with previous trends, the economy moved quite rapidly toward independence. In 1968 exports still covered a higher proportion of imports than could have been expected on the basis of previous trends. (This is true, however, only if defense imports are kept at their 1966 level.) While it is clear that the recession improved Israel's international trade position up to this point, the gains were not maintained in 1969, partly because the goals of policy shifted from economic independence toward maximizing economic growth, which led to substantially higher imports. But the 1969 retrogression was also affected by changed demand conditions in foreign markets for Israel's two main commodity exports – diamonds and citrus. It is clear from this historical experience that by reducing the standard of living moderately[28], by slowing economic growth, and by reducing defense expenditure, the Israeli economy, if it had to, could achieve rough balance in its international trade without catastrophic results.

Appendix: Imports and Exports of Services

While imports and exports of services accounted for 40 percent of the trade balance between 1965 and 1969, they were little affected by the recession (see Table 1 A).

Table 2A, which shows net imports and exports of services for the same period, indicates that, excluding the government's imports (mainly defense requirements), services exports exceeded services imports. The government deficit, however, grew very rapidly after the Six-Day War and pushed the services account into heavy deficit. The deficit on services account rose from 25 percent of the total import surplus in 1965 to 43 percent in 1969.

Unlike its widespread effects on commodity imports, the recession affected the growth rate of imports in only one services component, nonpassenger transportation. After increasing at an average annual rate of 16 percent during 1963–1965, it grew at a markedly slower 8.5 percent rate in 1966 and then fell 2.2 percent in 1967.[29] The decline resulted from the lower level of commodity imports

Table 1 A.

THE CURRENT ACCOUNT
(Millions of Dollars)

	1965	1966	1967	1968	1969
Imports					
Commodities	794.4	795.3	730.8	1,070.0	1,255.0
Services	474.9	521.7	749.3	846.8	956.0
Total	1,269.3	1,317.0	1,480.1	1,916.8	2,211.0
Exports					
Commodities	404.0	474.6	533.1	649.0	746.5
Services	344.9	397.5	416.2	549.6	571.2
Total	748.9	872.1	949.3	1,198.6	1,317.7

SOURCE: Bank of Israel, Annual Report 1969, p. 27.

69

Table 2A.   NET IMPORTS AND EXPORTS OF SERVICES: 1965-1969
                      (Millions of Dollars)

	1965	1966	1967	1968	1969
Transportation	54.4	54.9	61.1	71.5	72.8
Tourism	11.3	10.3	8.2	44.3	19.8
Insurance	-1.8	-2.1	-6.9	-4.1	1.1
Capital Services	-57.2	-58.7	-68.8	-70.5	-79.8
Miscellaneous Services	-9.6	5.1	-16.0	2.8	1.2
Total Excluding Government	-2.8	9.5	-22.4	44.0	15.1
Government Accounts*	-127.2	-133.7	-293.6	-333.1	-397.2
Total, Including Government Accounts	-130.0	-124.2	-316.0	-289.1	-382.1

*Net Government imports are probably grossly understated in these official figures. For security reasons, the Israeli government has been loath to disclose the volume of its arms imports.

SOURCE: Bank of Israel, Annual Report 1969, p. 44.

70

induced by the recession, which decreased total cargo transportation. In 1968, when commodity imports climbed sharply, nonpassenger transportation imports also shot up 30.8 percent.[30]

The major change in services imports which occurred during the 1965–1969 business cycle, the tripling of the level of defense imports, was unconnected with the recession policy. But the need for these higher defense imports did stimulate efforts toward the production of import substitutes in the years 1968–1969 and led to a substantial export of armaments. In 1970, according to the official figures, exports of the defense industries reached $50 million[31], the equivalent of 15 percent of industrial exports excluding diamonds. (The effects of higher defense spending on Israeli industry are discussed in Chapter 6.)

The most impressive growth in services exports during the 1965–1969 business cycle occurred in tourism and the concomitant expansion of passenger transportation services. While not connected with the recession, tourism has emerged as one of Israel's major growth exports — and one with a very high value-added component. In the years 1963–1966 tourism accounted for about $55 million of services exports.[32] Growth was very slow, rising from $53.4 million in 1963 to only $59.1 million in 1966.[33] After the Six-Day War, however, tourism became a year-round business as Israel's victory not only strengthened the emotional commitment of world Jewry to the nation but also greatly increased the tourist attractions available in it. The addition of the Old City of Jerusalem particularly enhanced Israel's potential as a tourist center. A further but decidedly minor factor was the November 1967 devaluation, which lowered the cost of visiting Israel, never inexpensive, by 16.67 percent. What seemed at first a transient burst of tourist enthusiasm leveled off into a steady flow of trade at considerably higher than prewar levels.

Tourism exports in 1968–1969 averaged $95.7 million, up 62 percent from 1966, the previous peak year. As a result of the larger number of tourists and the longer periods they spent in Israel, the year-round hotel occupancy rate in Israel rose to 60 percent in 1968, a 10 percent gain over 1966.[34] This surge brought with it large-scale investments which aided the economic recovery of the construction sector. In 1968, for example, 1,000 hotel rooms were added to the 14,000 already available, and an additional 2,500 rooms were planned for construction in 1969.[35]

1.   Bank of Israel, *Annual Report 1968*, p. 324.
2.   *Ibid.*
3.   *Ibid.*, pp. 325–326.
4.   Bank of Israel, *Annual Report 1969*, p. 271.
5.   Bank of Israel, *Annual Report 1969*, p. 7.
6.   *Ibid.*, p. 280.
7.   For lack of any other data, this paper uses the official figures for the level of defense spending, defense imports and defense exports. The official data can be assumed to be understated, but the extent of the bias is not known.
8.   Eliyahu Kanovsky, *The Economic Impact of the Six-Day War* (New York: Frederick A. Praeger, Inc., 1970), pp. 45–46.
9.   *Ibid.*, p. 46.
10.   *Ibid.*, p. 47.
11.   *Ibid.*, pp. 48–49. In 1970/71, defense expenditures soared to IL 5 million, fully 25 percent of GNP and 20 percent of total resources. See *The Jerusalem Post*, November 23, 1970, p. 9. These figures must be used with caution. As noted previously, they probably understate the actual level of defense expenditures. Some noted students of Middle Eastern affairs, for example, believe that defense spending in 1969/70 had already reached 25 percent of GNP.
12.   *The Jerusalem Post, loc. cit.*
13.   Kanovsky, *op. cit.*, pp. 69–70
14.   *The Jerusalem Post*, June 2, 1969, p. 11
15.   Bank of Israel, *Annual Report 1969*, p. 111.
16.   Kanovsky, *op. cit.*, pp. 115–116.
17.   *Ibid.*, p. 116.
18.   Bank of Israel, *Annual Report 1968*, pp. 35–39. See particularly page 37: "Analysis with the help of input-output coefficients likewise indicates that a considerable share of the incremental imports for current production was intended for stock replenishment. It also reveals that the process of building up stocks was largely completed in 1968."
19.   Although the official exchange rate in 1969 was IL 3.5 = $1.00, government subsidies made the effective exchange rate for exporters IL 4.20 = $1.00.
20.   Defense purchases are included under imports of services, not commodities.
21.   This is discussed in Chapter VII.
22.   See Paul Gaebelein, Jr., "Devaluation Under Full Employment and Inflation: The Case of Israel" (Unpublished Ph. D. dissertation, Department of Economics, Claremont Graduate School, 1967.)
23.   Bank of Israel, *Annual Report 1967*, p. 83.
24.   Abraham Subotnik, "The Development of an Econometric Model for Policy Decision-Making in Israel" (Unpublished Ph. D. dissertation, Department of Economics, Cornell University, 1967), pp. 179–180.
25.   Bank of Israel, *Annual Reports, 1968 and 1969*, pp. 44–45, 39 respectively. *The Jerusalem Post*, December 7, 1970. But if citrus and diamonds (which are affected by world market conditions) are excluded, as well as military exports (which were hampered by the needs of Israel's defense sector), then the balance of industrial exports rose by 18 percent.
26.   Central Bureau of Statistics, *Monthly Foreign Trade Statistics*, April 1970, Table 6, p. 29.
27.   See S. Reimer, "Israel: Ten Years of Economic Dependence," *Oxford Economic Papers*, XII (June, 1970); Eugene Van Cleef, "The Status of Israel – and a Look Ahead," *Middle East Journal*, Summer 1964; and Leonard

G. Rosenberg, "Industrial Exports: Israel's Requirements for Self-Support," *Middle East Journal*, Spring 1958.

28.   Per capita real GNP plus the import surplus fell only 5.2 percent between 1965 and 1967. This is certainly only a minor reduction in living standards.

29.   Bank of Israel, *Annual Report 1968*, p. 65.

30.   *Ibid.*

31.   *The Jerusalem Post*, November 23, 1970, p. 9.

32.   Bank of Israel, *Annual Report 1968*, p. 66.

33.   *Ibid.*

34.   *The New York Times*, February 23, 1969, p. IR 49.

35.   *Ibid.*

PART III

Internal Adjustments to Israeli Economic Policies

CHAPTER V

THE RESIDENTIAL CONSTRUCTION SECTOR

Realizing that in order to increase the real resources available to export industries the size of some other sectors had to be reduced, Israeli policymakers chose the residential construction sector as a prime target, for several reasons. First, its output could not be exported and did not increase the production potential of the economy. Secondly, as in most inflationary economies, there had been widespread speculation in real estate, to the detriment of the development of a capital market. Thirdly, the expected slowdown in immigration decreased the need for a large housing industry. The decision to reduce residential construction coincided with the end of the speculative boom in the private residential sector. Monetary and fiscal restrictions, as well as previous overbuilding in the private market, caused a sharp contraction of residential building from 1965 to 1967.

Housing has absorbed a large proportion of the Israeli economy's resources. "Unlike the United States and some other mature economies, housing is quite an important part of investment and does not receive residual resources; if anything, the opposite pattern is observed."[1] During the period 1952–1964 residential construction was the largest investment item, accounting for 34 percent of gross investment in fixed assets, and encompassed 9.5 percent of total employment as well as 8.0 percent of net domestic product.[2] In the early 1950's this was a direct consequence of mass immigration. Between 1948 and 1951 the population nearly doubled, creating vast housing needs. Abandoned Arab homes were only a partial and temporary solution to the housing shortage, because the immigrants had expectations of higher living standards and the government's development plans called for the building of new towns throughout the country.

Even after 1958, when the housing accommodation for the immigrants and the new towns were largely completed, housing activity did not slow appreciably. The proportion of GNP channeled into housing from 1959 to 1965 averaged 9.0 percent, only slightly lower than the 9.9 percent average for 1953–1958. Rapidly rising incomes, supplemented by large restitution receipts, enabled individ-

77

uals to raise the level of their housing accommodations, thus keeping residential construction a major part of domestic activity. An indication of rising housing standards is given by data on the median number of persons per room (excluding kitchens), which fell from 2.2 in 1957 to 1.7 in 1966.[3]

In this chapter I will briefly discuss the decline in public housing construction before tracing the course of the recession in private building to determine whether the policy objective of shifting resources out of the construction industry was achieved. Finally, I shall use an input-output analysis to show how the contractionary effects generated by the decline in residential construction freed real resources for other sectors.

Public Housing and Immigration

Public housing in Israel has been closely geared to changes in immigration. In the early years of the State the massive number of new arrivals forced the government to enter the housing market as a large-scale mass producer. Between 1950 and 1964, 64 percent of all residential units were built by the government, largely for immigrant housing.[4] The decline in real GNP growth in 1952–1953 and 1966–1967 reflects sharp declines in immigration and public housing as well as government policies aimed at fighting inflation.

This decline actually facilitated the policy of economic restraint which had been decided upon in late 1964.[5] When the Finance Minister's 1966/67 budget address announced an economic slow-down policy which called for shifting resources into export industries[6], the public sector could facilitate this movement of real resources by decreasing its own expenditures on immigrant housing. The amount of public housing started was cut back by a third from the 1964 level in 1965 and by an additional 55 percent in 1966 (see Chart 1 and Table 1); in 1966 it was less than a third as great as in 1964. The chief cut in the 1966/67 development budget was the drop in expenditures on new immigrant housing.

The Private Housing Market: 1962–1969

Beginning in 1961, the demand for housing mounted rapidly as the expectation of devaluation caused a flight from monetary assets into real assets.[7] The 1962 devaluation was followed by the large-scale conversion of foreign currency balances, primarily restitution payments, most of which were directed toward the purchase of housing and other consumer durables.[8] The rapid increase in demand pushed up housing prices sharply and, in turn, attracted local and foreign speculators hoping to reap quick and large capital profits. In 1962

78

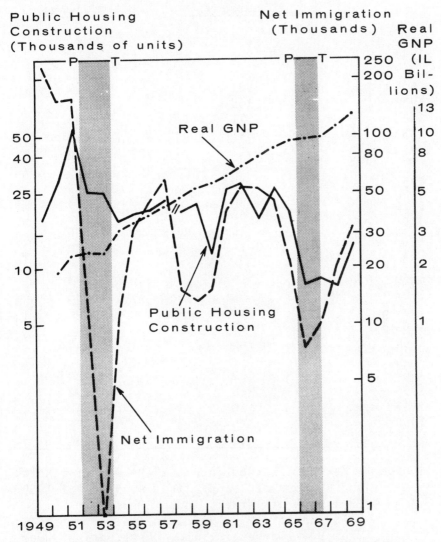

Chart 1

NET IMMIGRATION, REAL GNP
& PUBLIC HOUSING CONSTRUCTION

Public Housing
Construction
(Thousands of units)

Net Immigration
(Thousands)

Real
GNP
(IL
Billions)

Real GNP

Public Housing
Construction

Net Immigration

1949 51 53 55 57 59 61 63 65 67 69

Note: P and T are Peak and Trough for the
entire economy.
Source: Halevi and Klinov-Malul, The Economic
Development of Israel; Bank of Israel,
Annual Reports; Central Bureau of
Statistics, Monthly Bulletin of Statistics.

Table 1.   GNP, NET IMMIGRATION AND PUBLIC HOUSING

	Net Immigration (Thousands)	GNP (Constant IL Millions)
1949	232	
1950	161	1,927
1951	165	2,367
1952	11	2,495
1953	-1	2,476
1954	11	3,178
1955	32	3,502
1956	45	3,902
1957	60	4,336
1958	16	4,766
1959	14	5,330
1960	16	5,793
1961	41	6,366
1962	54	7,160
1963	53	7,929
1964	46	8,742
1965	22	9,480
1966	8	9,632
1967	10	9,740
1968	20	11,026
1969	33	12,404

SOURCE: Net Immigration data: 1949-1965 from Halevi
and Klinov-Malul, op. cit., p. 54; 1965-1969
from Bank of Israel, Annual Reports.
   GNP data: 1950-1963 data in 1963 prices
from Paul Gaebelein, Jr., "Devaluation Under
Full Employment and Inflation: The Case of
Israel" (Unpublished Ph. D. dissertation,
Department of Economics, Claremont Graduate
School, 1967), Table 24, pp. 247-248; 1964-

GNP (Percent Change)	Public Housing (# of Units)	Public Housing (Percent Change)
--	18,550	--
--	30,234	63.0
22.8	53,914	78.3
5.4	25,671	-52.4
-0.8	25,315	-1.4
28.4	18,274	-27.8
10.2	19,607	7.3
11.4	20,714	5.6
11.1	22,940	10.7
9.9	20,246	-11.7
11.8	22,282	10.1
8.7	12,029	-46.0
9.9	26,052	116.6
12.5	28,083	7.8
10.7	18,890	-32.7
10.3	27,300	44.5
8.4	18,980	-30.5
1.6	8,590	-54.7
1.1	9,120	6.2
13.2	8,410	-7.8
12.5	13,499	60.5

1969 data in 1964 prices from Central Bureau of
Statistics, Monthly Bulletin of Statistics (Jerusalem), March 20, 1970.
  Housing data: 1949-1957 data are public housing
units completed from Halevi and Klinov-Malul,
op. cit., p. 110; 1958-1969 data are public housing
units started from Bank of Israel, Annual Reports:
1959, p. 185; 1960, p. 179; 1961, p. 231; 1963,
p. 256 and Central Bureau of Statistics, loc. cit.

and 1963 a trade even developed in purchase contracts.[9] Home buyers also advanced their purchases because they expected prices to be higher later.

The Building Recession: Causes

The demand generated by these forces began to decline in 1963 as the reserves of accumulated foreign currency were used up and the rise in housing prices (65.4 percent from mid-1961 to mid-1963[10]) reduced their real value. In 1964 and 1965 demand was further restrained by a decline in the amount of restitution payments received; prices also rose and the speculative interest in housing decreased further.

To restrain the demand for housing, the government exercised its control over the public mortgage banks, which grant loans from government deposits earmarked for this purpose, and over some private financial institutions which grant mortgages using funds raised by issuing debentures in Israel and abroad. As Barnea explained,

> The mortgage banks' ability to raise capital depends on Government authorization for the floating of new security issues and a good part of sales depends on the Treasury's approving securities for purchase by the provident funds.[11]

In 1964 the approval of foreign debenture issues was restricted and limited to cases in which the Treasury had already committed itself.[12] In addition, government deposits in the public mortgage banks in 1965 were sharply reduced.[13] This action and a larger volume of loan repayments because prices were expected to rise rapidly reduced mortgage bank credit growth from IL 251 million in 1964 to IL 177 million in 1965.[14]

Despite weakening demand, rumors that the government intended to restrict new building as part of its program to release real resources for export industries[15] boosted housing starts in the first quarter of 1965 to 21 percent above the fourth quarter of 1964 (see Chart 2). When the government finally issued its order limiting building starts, the quota announced was so much larger than expected that much construction already begun was halted[16], leaving a large stock of housing, both completed and under construction, for which there was no demand. With its credit needs soaring as a result of this development, the construction industry was especially hurt by the tight monetary policy pursued by the Bank of Israel during 1964 and 1965 (see pp. 28–32). Commercial banks had no surplus liquid reserves and were unable to expand credit to meet the financing needs of builders. Moreover, because of the lower

Chart 2

RESIDENTIAL BUILDING AREA STARTED

(Quarterly Data, Seasonally Adjusted, Thousands of Square Meters)

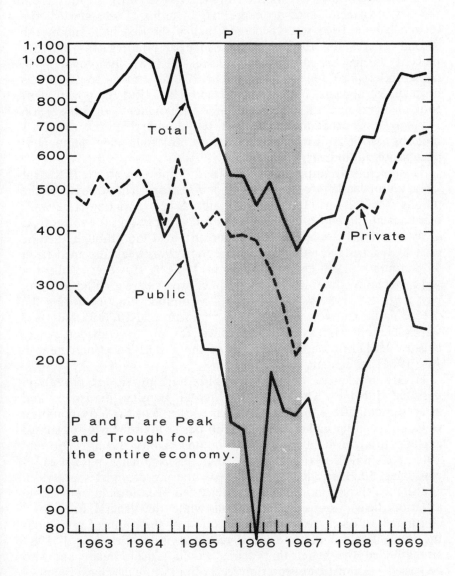

Source: Central Bureau of Statistics,
Monthly Bulletin of Statistics.

priority given construction than other economic sectors, the construction industry was not able to receive "directed" bank credit. The construction industry was thus forced to obtain its financing from the much higher priced bill brokerage market.[17] This further depressed the industry's profitability.

As Chart 2 shows, private housing activity declined steadily from the first quarter of 1965 to mid-1967. In terms of area started, the second half of 1965 was 28 percent below the first half, and by the second quarter of 1967 private residential building was only 31 percent as high as in the first quarter of 1965. Employment in construction also fell sharply — from 92,000 persons to 63,000, a drop of 32 percent, between 1965 and 1967. But the government took a hard line on construction unemployment. In June 1966 Finance Minister Sapir stated that ten thousand of the country's building workers would simply have to find new permanent occupations in industry.[18]

This decline in employment occurred despite the strong Histadrut labor unions and their emphasis on job security. The strength of the unions was demonstrated by their success in negotiating large wage increases at the end of 1965 for the following two-year contract. As a result, hourly wages rose 15 percent in 1966, though income earned declined because the construction workweek dropped from 41.8 hours in 1964 to 38.5 hours in 1967.[19] However, while the wage increases contained in the union contract were granted in 1966, payments to workers "on the side," a common practice during the preceding boom, were discontinued.[20] From mid-1966 to mid-1967 wages did not rise as much as called for in the contract, partly because Histadrut waived payment of the cost-of-living increment in July 1966 and January 1967.[21]

Private residential building was also hurt by slower growth in personal income. There is little rental housing in Israel, and improvement of accommodations has been one of the most common ways of spending higher incomes. But better housing involves a large capital outlay, and in the climate of uncertainty during 1966 and 1967, as individuals cut back their discretionary purchases of consumer durables, demand for new housing dropped sharply. In addition, although housing investment had been looked upon as an inflation hedge, housing prices fell while the general price level continued to rise, negating the attraction of this form of saving. As the intensification of the general recession in the first half of 1967 strengthened the belief that prices would remain steady and also increased pessimistic expectations regarding future earnings, financial assets were generally preferred to real assets.

Residential construction emerged from the recession more slowly than other sectors. The recovery which began in the second half of

1967 (see Chart 2) can be partly credited to the easing of the financing terms for home purchasers and to the bolstering of the financial position of builders. These financial incentives were aided materially by the changed psychological climate after the Six-Day War. In 1968 larger immigration, along with rising incomes as full employment was reached and overtime work increased, added to the demand. Personal restitution receipts also rose in 1967 and 1968. In 1968 private housing climbed 69 percent above its 1967 level, and by 1969 it had reached a new peak (see Chart 2). Public housing also rose substantially as immigration rebounded but was still far below its 1964 rate, largely because many of the immigrants were relatively well-to-do westerners and, unlike previous immigrants, could seek housing accommodations in the private market.

Even with the resurgence of housing in 1969, a permanent shift of resources out of this industry appears to have occurred, as was planned when the slowdown policy was originated. The total of residential building, in terms of area started, during 1969 was only 95 percent of the 1964 level, with public construction at 66 percent of its 1964 level and private construction at 118 percent of its 1964

Table 2.   CHANGE IN THE RELATIVE POSITION OF THE CONSTRUCTION INDUSTRY IN THE ISRAELI ECONOMY

	1969	1964	1955–1964 Average
Percent of Total Employment*	8.8	10.2	9.6
Percent of Gross National Product	5.6	9.1	9.4
Percent of Gross Fixed Investment	25.2	31.5	33.1

*Employment figures are for both residential and nonresidential construction workers. The other data refer only to residential construction.

SOURCE: Bank of Israel, Annual Report 1969; Halevi and Klinov-Malul, op. cit., pp. 110–111; Central Bureau of Statistics, Monthly Bulletin of Statistics.

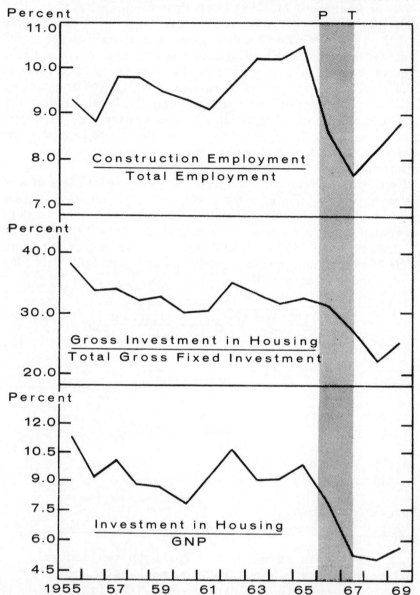

Chart 3
INDICATORS OF CONSTRUCTION ACTIVITY

Construction Employment
Total Employment

Gross Investment in Housing
Total Gross Fixed Investment

Investment in Housing
GNP

Note: P and T are Peak and Trough for the
entire economy.

Source: Halevi and Klinov-Malul, op. cit.,
Bank of Israel. Annual Reports.
and Central Bureau of Statistics,
Monthly Bulletin of Statistics.

86

level. The rise in the importance of the latter compared to public housing reflects not only the lower immigration, present and anticipated, but also the changed character of the current arrivals. The healthy 1969 residential construction industry had not in fact regained its former position as a sector in the economy, as shown by Table 2 and Chart 3.

Factors Accounting for the Relative Reduction in the Size of the Housing Sector

By European standards Israeli housing is still crowded[22], indicating that further income gains will be reflected in increased demand for better housing. Since the exodus of immigrants from over-crowded, low-quality public construction would normally replace heavy new immigration as a force sustaining a high level of demand for new private housing, one would expect a long lag between the decline of immigration and any decline in private residential construction. The fall in demand for private housing must therefore be related to the decline in real per capita income caused by the recession.

The decline in restitution payments, which fell IL 86.7 million from their peak level in 1963 to IL 330 million in 1966, also helped moderate the demand for private housing. Studies have found that 40 percent of restitution payments is spent on consumer durables.[23] If we assume (for want of more exact data) that the remainder is spent on housing, then the decline in restitution receipts decreased expenditures on housing by IL 52 million.

Slower income growth from domestic sources is undoubtedly the most important factor in the declining demand for housing. If disposable income from domestic sources had continued to grow during the recession at the same rate as during 1962–1965[24], it would have been IL 2154 million greater in 1967 than it actually was. Assuming that Israelis spend 20 percent of their income on housing[25], this lessened growth decreased expenditures on housing by IL 431 million, an amount 8.3 times larger than that induced by the decline in restitution payments. As demand slackened, the inventory of completed homes became excessive in relation to prospective sales. The drop in new building would not have been as drastic as it was, however, if there had not been speculative over-building and if the decline in demand had not coincided with restrictive monetary policies which compounded the financial problems of builders. Furthermore, the resurgence of private building in late 1968 and early 1969 showed that the decline in private housing was not due to underlying trends.

87

All of the output of residential construction goes to final destinations, and the demand for other products does not induce changes in residential construction.[26] Hence input-output analysis cannot explain changes in the demand for housing. But since a high proportion of the input into construction consists of domestic intermediates (building materials, electrical appliances, transportation, etc.), such an analysis can be extremely useful in exploring how the decline in residential building released resources in other sectors of the economy.

The share of domestic intermediates in residential construction is substantially higher than for the Israeli economy as a whole[27], and the sharp downturn in the housing sector therefore induced a significant contraction in other sectors, freeing resources for use in other industries. Table 3, using direct input coefficients, lists those industries which sell inputs directly to the construction industry and whose output was therefore affected through a cutback in orders. However, these direct coefficients do not show the total linkages of the construction sector, since changes in demand to its suppliers will cause these industries to change their demand for inputs from other branches. Table 4, using direct and indirect coefficients (the inverse matrix), shows the final results when the effects of all changes are taken into account. This analysis establishes the total industrial multiplier for housing at 1.7907.

Gross investment in residential construction fell by IL 608 million, at an annual rate, from the first quarter of 1965 to the second of 1967, in constant 1964 prices.[28] The inverse matrix indicates that this reduced total gross output of the economy by IL 1,089 million through the effects of this cutback on suppliers. While the construction industry itself imports few inputs, its suppliers do use imports to fill the demands of the housing industry. With an import coefficient of 0.1200[29], the decline in the housing sector would have reduced imports by IL 130.7 million at an annual rate by the middle of 1967.

Table 5 indicates that several suppliers experienced sharp contractions in output, wages paid, and employment as a result of the fall-off in demand from the construction sector. This is a partial equilibrium analysis which holds demand elsewhere in the economy constant, and the actual changes in output, wages paid, and employment in each of these industries could of course be higher or lower than those shown here because of the effects of changes in demand elsewhere in the economy. As Table 5 shows, the glass, ceramics, and cement industries were hardest hit, with gross output declining by IL 81.7 million. According to the wage coefficients in the input-output table and the indicated drop in output, workers in this industry experienced a decline in wage income of IL 24.2 million, and employment lessened by 1,600. Other important industrial suppliers which suffered severe contractions were mining, carpentry, chemicals and paints, petroleum, basic metals, metal products, machinery and electrical appliances; together their output was cut back by IL 198.3 million, wage income paid declined by IL 45.9 million, and employment was reduced by 3,300 persons.

In several industries which did not directly supply any inputs to residential construction there were large declines in demand because they did supply materials to building trades suppliers. For example, paper, cardboard, printing and publishing output dropped by IL 6.4 million[30], machinery output declined by IL 13.1 million, and electric power output required was reduced by IL 4.0 million.[31] Some other industries, like rubber and plastic products, experienced much greater declines through the secondary effects than from the direct effects of the cutback in orders from the housing industry.

The input-output analysis indicates that the decline in residential construction induced a cutback in total employment of 17,000 persons[32] or a drop in total employment of 2 percent from its 1965 level. The income effects are also significant, since many persons who did not become unemployed experienced shorter workweeks and periods of layoffs. The IL 270 million decline in wages caused by the decline in residential construction from early 1965 to mid-1967 was equal to 3.5 percent of the 1965 level of disposable private income from domestic sources. An income decline of this magnitude can be expected to restrain consumption and to release resources for exports.

Table 6 contrasts the actual change of gross industrial output in each of the supplying industries with the computed contraction of output ascribed to the decline in construction activity[33] and with changes in output induced by changes in export sales. The table shows that most of the industries which would have suffered a decline in output because of the contraction of construction actually experienced an increase, and that in most cases exports were an important factor in accounting for the difference. This further supports the contention that the contraction of construction did in fact allow for the expansion of industrial exports.

Table 3.   INDUSTRIES WHICH SUPPLY
              INPUTS TO THE RESIDENTIAL
              CONSTRUCTION SECTOR

Industries	Direct Input Coefficients
Agriculture	.0001
Mining	.0202
Wood Products and Carpentry	.1140
Paper, Printing and Publishing	.0005
Rubber and Plastic Products	.0006
Chemicals and Paints	.0159
Oil Refining	.0031
Cement, Glass and Ceramics	.1216
Basic Metals	.0432
Metal Products	.0296
Machinery and Electrical Equipment	.0102
Household Appliances	.0160
Transportation Equipment	.0009
Water and Irrigation	.0001
Land Transport	.0467
Other Transport and Communication Services	.0011
Services	.0652
Trade	.0198
Total Intermediate Inputs	.5086

SOURCE: This table is taken directly from the
          Bank of Israel's 1963 30 X 30 input-
          output table.   (Unpublished.)

Table 4. INDUSTRIES WHICH SUPPLY INPUTS
EITHER DIRECTLY OR INDIRECTLY TO
THE RESIDENTIAL CONSTRUCTION SECTOR

Industries	Input Coefficients
Field Crops	.0009
Livestock	.0002
Other Agriculture	.0007
Mining	.0293
Meat, Fish, Oil and Dairy Products	.0002
Other Food Products	.0009
Textiles and Apparel	.0084
Wood Products and Carpentry	.1423
Paper, Printing and Publishing	.0105
Leather and Leather Products	.0002
Rubber and Plastic Products	.0081
Chemicals and Paints	.0218
Oil Refining	.0180
Cement, Glass and Ceramics	.1344
Basic Metals	.0506
Metal Products	.0426
Machinery and Electrical Equipment	.0216
Household Appliances	.0203
Transportation Equipment	.0090
Residential Building	1.0007
Electric Power	.0066
Water and Irrigation	.0006
Land Transport	.0690
Shipping and Air Transport	.0006
Other Transport and Communication Services	.0110
Services	.1463
Trade	.0359
Total	1.7907

SOURCE: This table is taken directly from the
inverse matrix of the Bank of Israel's 1963
30 X 30 input-output table. (Unpublished.)

Table 5.   EFFECTS OF THE DECLINE IN
RESIDENTIAL CONSTRUCTION FROM 1965-I
TO 1967-II ON OTHER ECONOMIC SECTORS

	Decline in Output (IL Millions)	Decline in Wages	Decline in Employment
Mining	IL 17.8	IL 6.4	365
Textiles and Apparel	5.1	0.4	35
Wood Products and Carpentry	86.5	14.8	1,168
Paper, Printing and Publishing	6.4	1.2	94
Rubber and Plastic Products	4.9	1.0	69
Chemicals and Paints	13.3	3.1	197
Oil Refining	10.9	0.7	37
Cement, Glass and Ceramics	81.7	24.2	1,563
Basic Metals	30.8	8.1	494
Metal Products	25.9	7.5	586
Machinery and Electrical Equipment	13.1	2.6	206
Household Appliances	12.3	2.7	213
Transportation Equipment	5.5	1.4	91
Residential Construction	608.4	163.7	10,111
Electric Power	4.0	1.0	48
Land Transport	42.0	5.4	253
Other Transport and Communication Services	6.7	3.6	171
Services	89.0	19.0	1,131
Trade	21.8	3.3	196
TOTAL	1,086.1*	270.1	17,028

*The difference between this figure and the figure
in the text of IL 1,089 is due to excluding from the
table industries whose input coefficients were less
than .001.

92

Table 6. A COMPARISON OF THE ACTUAL CHANGE IN GROSS INDUSTRIAL OUTPUT WITH THAT INDUCED BY CHANGES IN RESIDENTIAL CONSTRUCTION AND EXPORTS, 1965 TO 1968

(IL Millions)

Supplying Industries	Actual Change in Gross Industrial Output	Output Change Caused by Decline in Residential Construction	Output Change Caused by Export Sales
Mining	85	-12.8	49.0
Textiles and Apparel	-205	-3.6	184.3
Wood Products and Carpentry	-113	-60.2	9.0
Rubber and Plastic Products	100	-3.3	9.0
Paper, Printing and Publishing	61	-4.1	15.3
Chemicals, Paints and Oil Refining	84	-17.6	138.2
Cement, Glass and Ceramics	121	-57.0	-0.4
Basic Metals	48	-25.9	13.6
Metal Products	67	-19.5	91.9
Machinery and Electrical Equipment and Household Appliances	362	-17.8	113.9
Transportation Equipment	301	-4.1	27.4
TOTAL	811	-222.5	651.2

SOURCE: Bank of Israel unpublished 1963 input-output table. Bank of Israel, Annual Report 1965 and 1968.

93

1. Michael K. Evans, *An Econometric Model of Part of the Israeli Economy* (Discussion Paper No. 86; Philadelphia: University of Pennsylvania), p. 10.

2. Nadav Halevi and Ruth Klinov-Malul, *The Economic Development of Israel* (New York: Frederick A. Praeger, Inc., 1968), pp. 110–111.

3. Economic Planning Authority, *Israel Economic Development, Past Progress and Plan for the Future* (Jerusalem, March 1968), p. 539.

4. *Ibid.*, p. 530.

5. In discussions I had with Jacob Arnon, Director of the Ministry of Finance and with David Horowitz, Governor of the Bank of Israel, in September 1969, they both said that the decision to embark on a slowdown policy was finally made in October 1964.

6. Pinchas Sapir, Minister of Finance, *Budget Address 1966/67* (Jerusalem, 1965).

7. Miriam Beham, *Monetary Aspects of the 1962 Devaluation* (The Maurice Falk Institute for Economic Research in Israel; Jerusalem, October, 1968), Chapter 3.

8. Evans, *op. cit.*, pp. 7 & 10.

9. Bank of Israel, *Annual Report 1964*, p. 284.

10. Bank of Israel, *Annual Reports 1963* and *1964*, p. 264 and p. 120, respectively.

11. Michael Barnea, "The Financial Structure of Israel's Mortgage Banks, 1958–1964," *Bulletin* (Bank of Israel, December 1965), p. 56.

12. *Ibid.*

13. Bank of Israel, *Annual Report 1965*, p. 389.

14. *Ibid.*, p. 372.

15. Bank of Israel, "Economic Developments in the First Half of 1965," *Bulletin* (Bank of Israel, December 1965), p. 13.

16. The quota was set as an average of the area of building starts from 1961–1963, the boom years of housing construction. See *Ibid.*

17. The only study to include bill brokerage in its analysis of credit allocation is Avigdor Steinberg, "Bill Brokerage in Israel, 1963–1967," *Bulletin* (Bank of Israel, March 1968). Steinberg found that the construction industry's credit consisted of 0.7 percent directed credit, 48.8 percent ordinary bank credit and 50.5 percent bill brokerage credit in June, 1967.

18. *The Jerusalem Post*, June 10, 1966, p. 1 and June 28, 1966, p. 2.

19. Central Bureau of Statistics, *op. cit.*, May 1969, Supplement, p. 7 (Hebrew).

20. Bank Leumi Le-Israel B.M., *Review of Economic Conditions in Israel* (New York: New York Branch, Bank Leumi Le-Israel, B. M., July 1966), special issue, p. 20.

21. See Bank of Israel, *Annual Report 1967*, Chapter 10 for more detail.

22. Economic Planning Authority, *op. cit.*, p. 539. Persons per room in 1965 (including kitchens): Israel, 1.25; West Germany, 0.87; Great Britain, 0.70; Norway, 0.75; Italy, 1.06.

23. See Evans, *op. cit.*, pp. 7 and 10.

24. Private disposable income from domestic sources grew at an average annual rate of 19.5 percent during the period 1962–1965 and by 7.1 percent per year 1966–1967. See Bank of Israel *Annual Reports*.

25. Housing expenditures averaged about 20 percent of consumer expenditures during 1960–1967. Economic Planning Authority, *op. cit.*, p. 25.

26. This statement abstracts from the income effect of changes in demand which will, of course, affect the demand for housing.

27. According to the Bank of Israel's unpublished 1963 input-output table, the share of intermediates in residential construction is 50.86 percent. Only

four other industries in the 30 x 30 table had as high or higher proportions of intermediates.

28. Central Bureau of Statistics, *op. cit.*, May 1969, p. 21.

29. Bank of Israel unpublished 1963 input-output table.

Note:

The employment effects generated by input-output techniques are heavily dependent on the assumed linear production function with constant factor proportions. While in the long run, an employer faced with a cutback in demand would adjust his use of capital and labor so as to be producing at the lowest point on his average cost curve at his new level of output, in the short run most of the adjustment must fall on labor. To a certain extent, therefore, the assumption that labor will decline in line with output is more readily acceptable for the short-run period analyzed here than it would be for a long-term analysis. The short run can be divided into three periods. In the first, the producer is unsure of why he is not receiving orders, and since he does not perceive any underlying longer-run trend, he discounts the momentary situation and continues producing at his former rate and building up inventory. In the second, he tries to cut production and inventory accumulation by cutting back on overtime or shortening the workweek. Since he has invested in the training of his workers, he is hesitant to lay off workers. However, in the third period, he does lay off workers in order to cut production further. Since input-output analysis assumes a linear relationship between output and employment, it will overstate the unemployment effects in the first two short-run periods and understate it somewhat in the third short-run period. While there is no reason to believe that the overstatements and understatements will balance and give a completely accurate picture, this is still the best way of determining how much of the employment changes in various industries resulted from a shift in demand for one industry at another stage in the production process.

30. The printing and publishing industry was affected because it sells its output to the food industry, to the textile industry, to the paper industry, to the rubber and plastic industry, to the basic chemicals and paints industry and to the oil and soap industry. Each of these industries supplies some inputs either to a building trades supplier or to residential construction firms. Pursuing the example further, the knitting and textiles industry uses some of the output of the printing and publishing industry. The knitting and textiles industry in turn sells some of its output to the carpentry industry — a building trades industry.

31. The figures in the text and in Table 5 are derived from calculations using the coefficients in the input-output tables.

32. As noted on page 84, total construction employment declined by 29,000 persons between 1965 and 1967. The input-output analysis indicates that 10,100 of these workers were employed in residential construction.

33. The figures in Table 6 showing the computed changes in output caused by the decline in residential construction differ from those in Table 5 in several respects. In Table 6, the computed change in supplying industries is based on an IL 382 million (in 1964 dollars) decline in residential construction from 1965 to 1968. The output declines due to residential construction were then inflated by the price changes experienced by individual sectors. (See Bank of Israel, *Annual Report 1968*, p. 254, for price changes by industry.) Table 5 by contrast shows output declines in 1964 dollars based on the annual rate decline of IL 608 million experienced by residential construction from 1965−I to 1967−II.

CHAPTER VI

THE INDUSTRIAL SECTOR

Many of the same cyclical factors operating in Israel's housing sector were also present in its industrial sector. Speculative over-investment during the years 1962 to 1964 led to surplus capacity in 1964 and 1965 and, consequently, to a decline in investment expenditures. The slowing of economic growth in 1965 and the recession during 1966 further intensified the decline in investment spending, since it made previous sales expectations excessively optimistic. The government's policies accentuated the cyclical movements by adding to the investment boom during 1962–1964 with large-scale investment projects and by cutting back sharply on development expenditures in 1965 and 1966, just when private investment had weakened considerably. Only in late 1966 and early 1967 did government investment policies become clearly counter-cyclical.

In contrast to its aim of reducing the size of the housing sector, the government's slowdown policy was aimed more at redirecting investment toward export industries than at permanently reducing the level of business fixed investment. The assumptions were that, by slowing the growth of domestic demand, export markets would become relatively more attractive and that the slack caused by the fall in domestic sales would be taken up by exports. It was hoped that when manufacturers were forced to meet foreign competition, they would increase productivity and the quality of products.

After describing some structural characteristics of Israeli industry, I shall discuss the role played by fiscal policy through the development budget and examine the forces acting within the private sector which caused the decline in investment from 1964 to 1967. The final section of this chapter deals with the changes induced in investment, industrial structure, and the trade balance by the recession.

The Structural Background

Some economists have concluded that Israel's problems are so severe that it cannot have a viable economy. For example, in the late 1950's the *Middle East Journal* published an analysis which stressed the inevitable dependence of Israeli production on imported inputs and argued that Israel would be unable to expand exports sufficiently to cover its import requirements.

Economic activity in Israel almost universally consumes foreign currency, whether it is the fuel that runs the transportation system, the electricity (generated by burning imported crude oil) that keeps factories in operation or provides the energy for the water pumping stations on Israel's expanded irrigation network. The bulk of the raw materials that are processed in Israel's numerous industrial establishments, as well as the machinery and equipment that perform the actual processing, are paid for in scarce foreign exchange. The structure of Israel's economy makes certain that when industrial production does increase, the foreign exchange component of this output will be significant.[1]

The article concluded that imported inputs would not provide the basis for the necessary level of exports because "industrially inexperienced Israel does not have the technical, managerial or marketing skills for the needed expansion in industrial exports."[2] As recently as 1964, another article in the *Middle East Journal* maintained basically the same position.

Israel's industrial future is limited not only by its shortage in mineral deposits, but also by its inability to import to advantage raw materials for processing and re-export, and by a restricted market for its products.... [Moreover] foreign businessmen who would trade with Israel are faced with risks growing out of international antagonisms.[3]

The necessity of channeling a large proportion of production into exports if a high standard of living is to be maintained is underscored by Israel's small size. As Moshe Mandelbaum has argued:

The most serious limitation on industrial growth seems to be the small (though growing) local market. Israel's total area is approximately 8,000 square miles. Its population was only 1.9 million in 1956 and 2.3 million in 1962. This tiny scale of the local market made it uneconomical to develop many industrial activities which require substantial economies of scale. Such activities could become profitable only if an export market would become available. But under the existing conditions the export market was hardly advantageous.[4]

Yet neither a small home market nor a paucity of natural resources has prevented several European countries from being active trading nations and attaining high living standards. A more important factor, and one which is sometimes only obliquely mentioned, is that

97

the institutional structure of the Israeli economy prevents imported inputs from being exported profitably. This difficulty explains Mandelbaum's statement that existing Israeli conditions made the export market hardly advantageous. High tariffs and large subsidies have allowed inefficient economic units to survive and multiply and have enabled high cost firms to expand both domestic sales and exports. Industrial development has proceeded at a rapid pace only with substantial government support, which, to an extent varying with the manufacturing activity involved, has created artificial incentives for production, sometimes at considerable economic cost.

Citing statistics showing Israel's rapid growth in industrial production and in exports does not negate these criticisms, nor does it reveal whether Israel is heading toward a balanced current account. Thus, it is possible for all four of the following statements to be true. 1) Industrial production grew at a very rapid 10.9 percent annual rate from 1950 to 1965, and at 13.5 percent a year from 1960 to 1965. 2) During the 1960's industry and mining absorbed an increasing part of total investment expenditures and became the most important branch of the economy, accounting for 25 percent of total employment and of net domestic product. 3) Industry has been able to divert an increasing share of its output to exports: industrial exports grew at a 18.5 percent annual rate between 1960 and 1965, far faster than the growth in industrial output.

> 4)...industrial expansion is very much the result of virtually complete protection; consequently it is very difficult to ascertain how much of Israel's industry has developed along lines of present — let alone future — comparative advantage, or what dislocation will eventuate when industry has to face international competition.[5]

Tariffs are obviously a crucial factor here. Following the devaluation of the Israeli pound in 1962, administrative protection was increasingly replaced by fiscal protection. Whereas in 1962 most imports were controlled directly, by 1968 about 90 percent of total imports were virtually free from quantitative restrictions. Customs duties were set at high enough levels, however, to ensure the existence of all the enterprises presently operating in the economy. The average customs duty for industrial output in 1965 was a high 121 percent, with a quarter of production receiving protection at rates exceeding 225 percent.[6] As Table 1 shows, considerable differences exist among the main branches in the average rate of customs duty levied, which ranged from 200 to 230 percent in the transport equipment and textile branches to 35—40 percent for nonmetallic minerals and chemical production.

Because tariff rates were set at levels which ensured the continued

Table 1.   AVERAGE RATE OF CUSTOMS DUTY
PER MAIN BRANCH

Branch	Branch Average	Weight in Total Industrial Output
Foodstuffs and Tobacco	79	19.5
Textiles	231	8.5
Clothing	178	10.3
Wood and Carpentry	60	8.3
Paper and Paper Products	50	5.3
Leather and Footwear	130	2.9
Rubber and Plastics	55	3.0
Chemicals	40	6.8
Oil Refining	40	3.6
Nonmetallic Minerals	35	5.1
Basic Metals	37	2.8
Machinery and Electrical Equipment	48	4.4
Household Equipment and Miscellaneous	69	4.3
Transport Equipment	201	5.9
TOTAL	121	100.0*

*Excluding the diamond industry.

SOURCE: Flora Davidov, "The Liberalization of
Imports – February 1962 to May 1965,"
Bulletin (Bank of Israel, April 1966), p. 53.

existence of all operating firms, the major aim of the liberalization program – improving the efficiency of industry – was thwarted. Import liberalization had been intended as a means of achieving better factor utilization in the economy as a whole and necessarily involved the diversion of productive factors from one branch or enterprise to another, which is very liable to entail the closing of individual firms. An unwillingness to allow this shift to occur has created continued inefficiency in Israeli production.

High tariff protection has hindered efficient production by enabling small, high cost firms to survive. In fact, Israeli industry is largely composed of such small privately owned firms. In 1965 only 320 firms (1.3 percent of the establishments) employed 100 persons or more, and one need only walk through any of the industrial sections of Israeli cities to be impressed with the minute size of many of these enterprises. There are hundreds of "industrial" shops in twenty foot store fronts, employing two or three men turning out consumer goods or repairing machines. Thus, much of Israeli industry is actually handicrafts.

While the main explanation for the survival of such shops is found in the high level of tariffs, one may also wonder why they are not competitively forced out of business by the larger firms which should have lower costs as a result of the division of labor and economies of scale. An important factor here is the ability of the small shops to offset the lower costs of true industrial production by not paying Histadrut wage levels. While virtually the entire labor force is nominally covered by the national wage agreements, in practice this is not possible in a nation of tiny enterprises. Only the larger firms (which account for most exports) pay Histadrut wages. Thus, lower productivity is partly offset by the workers' acceptance of lower wage rates because their take-home pay is often not lower, and may actually be higher, than that in the larger firms. This discrepancy arises when the small shops do not withhold income tax payments.[7] By ignoring these lapses, the government is, of course, providing such firms with a substantial, if indirect, subsidy.

While these small firms do produce goods for the domestic market, they are unable to provide exports. Ignoring for the moment their high production costs, they produce too small a total volume either to make the expense of establishing overseas contacts worthwhile or to attract foreign buyers to them. Thus the limited labor resources are drawn into firms without any export potential, while firms with export capabilities are competitively handicapped by Histadrut's wage and labor policies and the government's high income tax rates.

At the other extreme, and despite the presence of a large number of tiny firms, production in many fields is quite concentrated, especially in those requiring heavy capital investments. The Israeli government has not adopted the American attitude toward competition; in fact, it has encouraged producers' organizations to form and to allocate the market among their members.[8] But since oligopolies and cartel arrangements are not conducive to cost cutting efforts, the government's attempts to create firms of an economic size without exposing them to foreign competitive pressures have kept Israeli costs high.

Cartel arrangements have been used by the government to promote exports through the establishment of equalization funds. Five autonomous funds — in cotton textiles, wool textiles, plywood, leather, and agriculture — are designed to ensure a high return to the producer for his exports at the expense of lower profits on domestic sales. For example, in the plywood industry the exporter receives an export premium which is financed through an equalization fund created by levies on raw materials for plywood production destined for domestic consumption. Since the rates of assistance differ for various industries, they apparently give greater encouragement to the less efficient industries. The agricultural and textile funds often operate at a deficit, which is then financed from the government budget.

The government accelerated the growth rate of industry not only by providing a protected home market but also by granting far-reaching incentives to investors. Development Budget loans and a variety of tax incentives have encouraged industrial investment, in certain instances primarily to provide employment opportunities or to develop remote areas. Some uneconomic or marginally viable undertakings have resulted. When exports have received direct government subsidies and indirect assistance in the form of reductions in raw materials costs or favorable terms on loans to meet operating and investment requirements, to the degree that such support has raised the dollar return on privately invested capital per dollar of export sales, the measures have been equivalent to a devaluation. But, unlike a devaluation, they have involved cumbersome administrative procedures which increased the scope of the bureaucracy in the workings of the economy. More importantly, they have made it very difficult, if not impossible, to calculate the actual cost to the economy of these investments. Thus, in a more indirect form, the loans, tax incentives, and subsidies have created all the inefficiencies of a multiple exchange rate system.

Under the Law for the Encouragement of Capital Investments, "approved enterprise" status is granted to new firms which export at least half of their output or to existing enterprises which expand by 50 percent and undertake to export at least half of the additional output. Approval entitles an enterprise to substantial tax reductions as well as access to government loans and grants, which may together total as much as 80 percent of the proposed investments.[9] The government program assumes that these investments would not be made on purely economic grounds and that tax and loan incentives are necessary to alter the cost structure facing the private investor. Since variable as well as fixed costs are lowered by government aid, it is not clear whether firms receiving such aid would be economically viable in the context of Israeli cost relationships without continuing government help.

While these incentives have undoubtedly increased investment in industry, they have not clearly been able to increase industrial exports as intended. Despite the fact that some industries only qualified for "approved" status because they agreed to export a high proportion of their output, in practice it has been impossible to enforce this provision. One study comparing the export performance of firms which received loans from the Development Budget with those which did not found that there was only a small difference in their proportion of output exported. In 1963 the group receiving loans exported only 12.8 percent of its output, while the group not receiving government loans exported 8.5 percent.[10]

Tariff protection enabled Israeli manufacturers to get higher prices in the Israeli market than they could get by exporting. As long as domestic demand was strong, there was little spur for the difficult task of establishing export markets and of trying to lower costs so that exports would be profitable. While industrial exports did grow rapidly, most export gains came in industries which marketed all of their goods abroad, rather than from industries which would have had to divert some of their productive capacity from satisfying the home market.

The structure of the Israeli labor market, especially its unionization, keeps production costs high and impedes the effectiveness of anti-inflationary policies. With Histadrut's membership as large as three-quarters of the civilian work force[11], it plays a central role in determining wage levels and working conditions. Critics of Israeli wage policies have focused on both the high level of wages and the cost-of-living allowance as sources of unjustified inflation and economic distortions. Higher wage levels have distorted the whole Israeli production mix by causing the more capital-intensive methods of production to be preferred. Moreover, the high labor costs were matched by excessively low capital costs to private investors as a result of the government's subsidies for investment. High wage levels not only increased the demand for capital goods but also restricted the resources available for investment. For the higher the wage level, the lower generally will be the share of resources that can be diverted from current consumption to investment.

The fact that in the Israeli economic system wages are tied to a cost-of-living index creates further problems. When the demand for labor is excessive, payment of the cost-of-living allowance not only accelerates price and wage increases but also raises costs uniformly among various branches which do not profit equally from inflation. Although wage rises would eventually tend to be equalized throughout the economy, equalizing in advance produces pressures from the marginal firms on the government to expand the money supply.

The allowance is also an obstacle to successful devaluation, which usually aims at reducing the import surplus by raising the price of imports relative to domestic goods and by decreasing aggregate demand. When real wages are kept constant, profits must be curtailed and unemployment increased if total demand is to be reduced. An anti-inflationary increase in sales and excise taxes poses a similar problem: the rise in prices automatically raises wages, so that as far as employees are concerned the tax cannot achieve its objective of lowering nominal incomes.

Histadrut employment practices have also contributed to the high production costs of the Israeli economy. The fact that it is virtually impossible to fire workers has led to labor padding, especially in the larger establishments and in the government. A 1965 International Labor Office report on manpower assessment and planning mentioned:

> One of these [institutional factors] is the difficulty of separating surplus workers from payrolls, rooted in the welfare ideology of the State and the employment market conditions which existed during its early years. Under existing agreements a worker regarded unsatisfactory may be dismissed during the first 90 days of his employment. Thereafter, he becomes a permanent employee and may be dismissed only for just cause.[12]

The Role of the Development Budget

During the years of rapid growth in the early 1960's a significant proportion of investment spending was connected with four huge government investment projects: Ashdod port, the National Water Carrier, electricity installations in Ashdod and Haifa, and the expansion of the Dead Sea Works. The port at Ashdod essentially entailed building an entire new city, with housing, roads, commercial centers, and other structures to accommodate the port workers who moved there; the population rose from 4,600 in 1961 to 27,000 in 1966. The National Water Carrier, a large system of pipes and pumping stations constructed to bring water from the north to irrigate farms in the South, involved a similarly vast effort. Expanding the large complex of plants which extract phosphates, nitrates, and other minerals from the Dead Sea, process them, and prepare them for export was also a multi-million dollar project. (Israel is one of the world's major phosphate exporters.) The National Water Carrier and the electric power stations were completed in 1964, and the two other projects during 1965.

Despite the fact that government expenditures on these development projects had accounted for approximately 15 percent of nonresidential capital spending during the years 1962 to 1965 (see Table 2), little attention was given at the time to the deflationary impact their completion would have on the economy. It was partly because the projects had not been undertaken as discretionary fiscal policy actions that they were not viewed in that light.[13] In line with the slowdown policy announced in the 1966/67 budget address, the government did, however, deliberately defer or shelve "marginal

Table 2.

GROSS FIXED NON-DWELLING INVESTMENT
(IL Millions; in Current Prices)

	1962	1963	1964	1965	1966	1967	1968	1969
Government Development Projects	163	229	257	314	307	294	294	313
Government Expenditures on Public Buildings	167	218	274	329	321	311	381	431
Total Government	330	447	531	643	628	605	675	744
TOTAL	1,255	1,455	1,892	1,952	1,613	1,401	2,159	2,776
Government Development as % of Total	13	16	14	16	19	21	14	11
Total Government as % of Total	26	31	28	33	39	43	31	27
% Change in Total Government		35	19	21	-2	-4	12	10
% Change in Total		16	30	3	-17	-13	54	29

Note: Government development projects taken as purchases on capital account for economic services, 1965-1969; 1962-1964: purchases on capital account for roadbuilding, the National Water Carrier, postal and transport enterprises.

SOURCES: Bank of Israel, Annual Reports 1963, pp. 122, 248; 1964, p. 156; 1965, pp. 166, 283; 1966, pp. 180, 317; 1967, pp. 119, 192, 329; 1968, pp. 99, 157, 268; 1969, pp. 80, 123, 228.

development activities" in 1966 in order to reduce government spending and "ease the demand for labor."[14]

Increased government spending on public buildings also added to demand pressures during the boom years (see Table 2) and in 1965, as part of its slowdown policy, the government limited the amount of new public building started. As a result, expenditures on public buildings fell in 1966. Once again its actions strengthened the swing in the cycle.

As Table 2 shows, investment under public control rose on average by 25 percent each year from 1963 to 1965. In 1966, as the economy descended into a severe recession, public investment fell 22 percent. (As a percentage of total investment, public investment rose from 1965 to 1967, because private investment fell rapidly during these years.) While this cutback in public investment was primarily intended to allay demand pressures, certain financing problems did to some extent force them. In 1966 the government's ability to finance investment was curtailed by the ending of reparations payments from Germany and by a lower level of unilateral and bond receipts from abroad (see Table 3). Partly as a result of this 30 percent decline in its own receipts in 1966, the Israeli government slowed its rate of lending to the public in that year (see Table 4). Since the development budget is the most important source of long-term credit for investments by the private sector, the growth rate of private investment was unavoidably cut. Development budget policies are also furthered by a "direct credits program" carried out by the Bank of Israel, which, according to Governor Horowitz, were determinedly kept below the allowable maximum in an effort to help the government cut back on private investment spending.[15]

The Cycle in Private Business Investment

After the 1962 devaluation, the government imposed price controls on industrial goods to prevent rising consumer income and liquidity from bidding up prices. The rapid growth in personal income, coupled with the price freeze which further increased real income in terms of industrial goods, created a heavy demand for industrial products, which, in turn, stimulated investment to meet the growing demands. Higher domestic demand was also met by diverting industrial exports to the domestic market. Thus demand pressures were expressed not in higher prices but in greater capital outlays, reduced exports, and increased imports.

Investment in machinery received further impetus from the need to offset rising wage costs for which higher prices could not compensate fully. Although the price freeze was accompanied by a wage freeze, average monthly wages rose by 12 percent in 1963 and

105

Table 3.   FOREIGN TRANSFERS TO THE PUBLIC SECTOR
(Millions of Dollars)

	1962	1963	1964	1965	1966	1967	1968	1969
Reparations from West Germany	47.0	28.4	16.9	16.7	-2.0	--	--	--
United States Grants-in-Aid	8.0	5.9	8.2	4.7	3.0	--	--	--
Unilateral Transfers (Jewish Agency)	71.8	83.0	93.2	104.6	103.4	321.8	162.6	179.1
Independence and Development Loans (Net)	13.1	10.6	24.5	33.3	11.3	171.5	79.2	63.3
TOTAL	139.9	127.9	143.0	159.3	113.0	493.3	241.8	242.4

SOURCE: 1961-1963 from Bank of Israel, Annual Report 1963, p. 44, 46;
1964-1965 from Bank of Israel, Annual Report 1965, p. 58;
1966 from Bank of Israel, Annual Report 1966, p. 73;
1967-1968 from Bank of Israel, Annual Report 1968, pp. 68, 70;
1969 from Bank of Israel, Annual Report 1969, p. 48.

106

Table 4.   NET LOANS GRANTED BY THE PUBLIC SECTOR

	IL Millions	Percent Change
1962	414	17.3
1963	403	-2.7
1964	455	13.6
1965	499	9.0
1966	508	1.8
1967	724	42.5
1968	865	19.5
1969	939	8.6

SOURCE: Bank of Israel, Annual Reports 1964, p. 127; 1966, p. 146; 1969, p. 104.

1964[16] because of increases in the cost-of-living allowance, larger fringe benefits, and unofficial compensation to attract and keep labor in a tight labor market. As Table 5 shows, such investment surged under these conditions, rising 11 percent in 1963 and 18 percent in 1964, in constant prices. Expansion of productive facilities at such rates would inevitably outstrip expected increases in domestic demand, even if the population and income had continued rising at their current high rates. Such rapid expansion in capacity was certainly felt to be excessive in 1965, when immigration slowed sharply and a fall in restitution payments cut the growth rate of disposable income.

As a result of the sharp increase in industrial capacity created by high investment spending in the previous two years and the slower growth of sales in 1965, investment spending in 1966 was sharply reduced. Investment in machinery fell 12 percent below the 1965 peak (see Table 5). Almost 30 percent of the decline in investment in machinery and equipment reflects the collapse of the construction sector. Investment in machinery by the building industry averaged IL 60 million in both 1964 and 1965 but fell to IL 22.5 million in 1966 and to IL 6.9 million in 1967.[17]

Inflationary pressures after the 1962 devaluation also found an outlet in speculation in real estate. As urban land prices soared, industrial and commercial firms were able to finance much of the cost of purchasing new premises in new centers by selling their old buildings at large profits.[18] This led to a surge in speculative building, with developers depending on the buyers' ability to purchase their new premises by selling their old ones. The results of this building activity became apparent only in 1964, when industrial

107

Table 5. INVESTMENT IN MACHINERY AND EQUIPMENT*

	IL Millions (At 1969 Prices)	Percent Change
1962	555	
1963	617	11
1964	729	18
1965	797	9
1966	698	-12
1967	558	-20
1968	883	58
1969	1,199	36

*Excluding investment in ships, aircraft and automotive vehicles.

SOURCE: Bank of Israel, Annual Reports 1965, p. 85; 1969, p. 81.

building completions rose 18 percent and commercial buildings completed surged 88 percent[19], increases which far exceeded any reasonable expectation of the rise in demand. After many contractors found themselves with a stock of unsold buildings, new commercial and industrial building starts dropped sharply during 1965, but the completion of buildings in the process of construction further enlarged the surplus (see Chart 1). In 1966 new commercial construction plummeted to two-thirds of its 1964 level, while industrial building starts fell to a level only one-third as high as in 1964.[20]

The decline in new nonresidential construction had little to do with the government regulations issued in January 1965, which ordered a complete halt to the construction of office and business premises but included no restrictions on industrial building. Nevertheless, industrial building starts fell more rapidly than did commercial building. Moreover, when the government restrictions were removed in February 1966, building starts continued to drop rapidly.

The restrictive directives issued during the years of rapid growth did not further the government's goals of expanding exports. If anything, they had the perverse effect of increasing the activity they were designed to limit. Price controls made industrial goods relatively cheaper than other consumer goods and raised domestic demand for them at the expense of industrial exports. The wage freeze, since it was not accompanied by limitations on economic growth, was not

Chart 1

COMMERCIAL AND INDUSTRIAL BUILDING

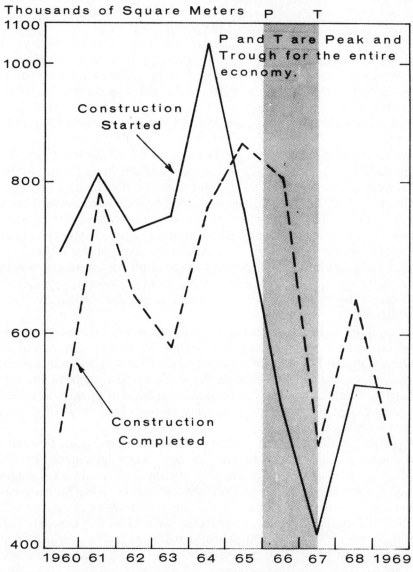

Thousands of Square Meters

P and T are Peak and Trough for the entire economy.

Construction Started

Construction Completed

Source: Central Bureau of Statistics, Statistical Abstract of Israel 1967, and Bank of Israel, Annual Report 1969.

effective. Moreover, because it was used as a justification for industrial price controls, its effect was to squeeze industrial profits and reduce the attractiveness of investment in industry. (An indication of this is the much greater rise in non-industrial shares on the Tel Aviv stock exchange than in industrial stocks.[21]) Since export prices were stable in the early 1960's, profitability could not be enhanced by diverting sales to exports.

The marked slowing in monetary expansion and the decline in liquidity during 1964 and 1965 also played a part in reducing investment. During 1962–1963 large foreign currency inflows, which the Bank of Israel did not sufficiently offset, pushed the money supply up by an inflationary 52 percent. The Bank succeeded in moderating money supply growth to 14 percent in 1964 and to only 9 percent in 1965 (the slowest money supply growth since the establishment of the State) by raising reserve requirements and by not allowing banks to use their full quota of directed credits. During the closing months of 1965 and through the first quarter of 1966, monetary restraint was sufficiently restrictive to cause an actual decline in the money supply. This drove up the interest rate on bank negotiated bills[22], making investments more costly. Further evidence that the decline came from restrictive monetary policies rather than from a slackening of loan demand is given by the continued rise in the velocity of money during these months (velocity peaked in March 1966)[23] and by the sharp rise in the bill brokerage trade (which rose 29 percent in 1966).[24]

The Bank of Israel was aided in its efforts to dry up loanable funds for investment financing by the decline in foreign private capital inflows. Foreign capital inflows reached a peak in 1964 and then, in response to the fall in prices on the stock exchange and in the real estate market as well as the decline in economic growth, dropped rapidly thereafter. They stood at only 16 percent of their 1964 level by 1967.[25]

A substantial decline in profits in 1966 also depressed investment demand. In early 1966 Histadrut's new wage agreement for the following two years called for a 15 percent increase in basic wages over a two-year period, in addition to cost-of-living adjustments every six months. In January 1966 the cost-of-living allowance was raised 9.3 points, increasing the total wage bill by 7 percent. This increase on top of the 5–10 percent basic wage increases which went into effect in early 1966 caused unit labor costs to soar in 1966 (see Chart 2).

The timing of the wage increases just after the peak of the business cycle was particularly inopportune, since they shot costs up when sales were falling. The resulting cuts in output and employment, by reducing capacity utilization rates and slowing productivity gains,

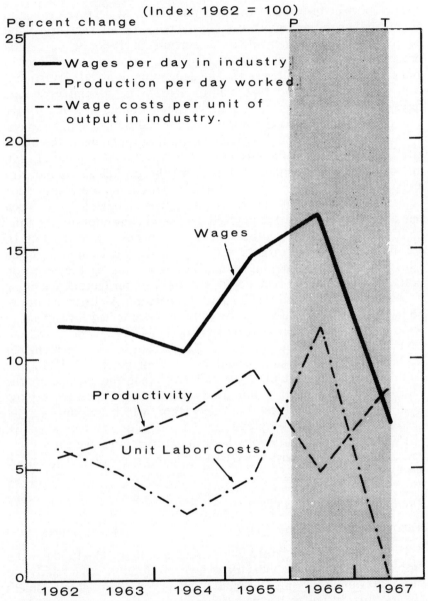

Chart 2
PRODUCTIVITY,
WAGES AND UNIT LABOR COSTS
(Index 1962 = 100)

Percent change

- Wages per day in industry.
- Production per day worked.
- Wage costs per unit of output in industry.

Wages

Productivity

Unit Labor Costs.

Note: P and T are Peak and Trough for the entire economy.
Source of basic data: Bank of Israel, Annual Report.

depressed profits further. The share of profits in national income fell from its 1962—1965 average of 15.4 percent to 4.4 percent in 1966[26], a drop which could only lead to sharp cutbacks in new investment.

The drop in investment in 1966 was the most decisive change in domestic demand and markedly contracted economic activity. Total nonresidential investment fell 15 percent in 1966, while capital outlays by the industrial and construction sectors were reduced 25 and 65 percent, respectively.[27] The depression in private investment continued through the first half of 1967. The general economic recession depressed demand, and the stock of idle new machinery and unsold buildings curtailed the need for additional capital outlays.

According to the Bank of Israel's input-output tables, the direct effect of the decline in business fixed investment was an IL 450 million decline in income payments by the capital goods industry and its suppliers from 1965 to 1967.[28] This alone represents a 5.3 percent contraction in national income from its 1965 level. When one adds the effects of the induced decline in consumption, the total multiplier effect of the cutback in capital spending is an IL 1 to IL 1.5 billion reduction in gross national product between 1965 and 1967.[29] If private investment had not fallen during the recession years, the national product would have risen (other factors remaining unchanged) by an additional 10 to 15 percent. As Bregman notes, "Since it [GNP] actually rose by only 3 percent, had investment in 1966 and 1967 remained at its level of 1964—1965, the growth of GNP would have amounted to 13—18 percent, or 7—9 percent per annum, and no recession would have taken place."[30] Using the Bank's input-output tables, he estimates that the decline in the value-added component of non-dwelling investment reduced employment by 61,000 workers. Unskilled labor, which accounts for 61 percent of all workers employed in the production of capital goods, was hardest hit[31], primarily because of the large weight of the construction sector, with its relatively high proportion of unskilled workers, in investment.[32]

The Effects of the Recession

Wages, Prices, and Productivity

A 1969 report by the World Bank concluded that "The fundamental problem facing Israel's industry is high production costs relative to those prevailing in international markets."[33] Throughout Israel's history this difficulty has necessitated the elaborate system of high tariffs and export subsidies described in the previous section. The recession, by stabilizing wages and prices and by leading to the laying off of redundant workers, sharply improved the competitive position

112

of Israeli industry. Furthermore, by reducing the growth of domestic sales, it made those industries which could export relatively more profitable, thus adding to their attractiveness as investment opportunities. The government enhanced the effects of the recession by imposing a wage-price freeze during 1968 and 1969, by cutting tariff protection, and by increasing its aid to export industries.

Wages in manufacturing and mining rose 49.7 percent between 1961 and 1965, somewhat less than the general rise in wages of 56.2 percent during this period.[34] This was considerably more rapid than wage increases in Israel's major export markets (see Table 6). As a result, Israeli labor costs rose 16.6 percent relative to labor costs in her major export markets. Without taking into account changes in productivity, differences in labor costs do not necessarily indicate alterations in competitiveness; but movements of this magnitude can be taken to indicate at least some relative deterioration in the competitiveness of Israeli exports because of higher labor costs.

The recession did not have an immediate impact on wages, because new wage agreements, negotiated in late 1965, went into effect in

Table 6.　　WAGE INCREASES IN ISRAEL AND IN
ISRAEL'S MAJOR EXPORT MARKETS
(Percent Change)

	Israel	Israel's Major Export Markets	Relative Change in Israeli Labor Costs (1961 = 100)
1962	11.2	7.6	103.3
1963	11.1	6.8	107.5
1964	10.2	8.2	109.5
1965	14.2	7.3	116.6
1966	16.1	7.2	126.2
1967	5.4	6.0	125.5
1968	3.0	7.3	120.5
1969	3.6	8.0	115.5

Note: The data for the export markets are unweighted averages of wage changes in the United States, the United Kingdom, Germany, Holland, Belgium, France, Japan and Switzerland.

SOURCE: International Monetary Fund, International Financial Statistics, Supplement (Washington, D. C., 1971).

early 1966. As a result, wages rose another 16 percent during 1966, despite increased unemployment. All the growth in daily wages, however, occurred during the first half of the year, primarily during the first three months of 1966. After the average monthly wage per employee peaked in September, it began to decline, and by May 1967 it was 5.3 percent lower than in September 1966. With the renewal of economic growth in the second half of 1967, average monthly wages began to rise slowly, but the average for the year remained virtually the same as in 1966. A wage freeze agreed to by Histadrut in 1968 and substantial unemployment kept the rise in industrial wages to a bare 3 percent in 1968. After 1967 the 1968 rate of wage gain was the slowest of the 1960's. As Table 6 indicates, the relative wage stability enjoyed by Israel during the economic recovery, while inflationary trends were accelerating in many of its export markets, considerably decreased the relative costliness of Israeli labor.

Less rapid wage advances and continued gains in output per worker also reversed the rise in unit labor costs. Changes in that area serve as an indicator of the competitive strength of Israel both in the export market and in the domestic production of import substitutes. As Table 7 shows, the Israeli decline in unit labor costs was not matched in the major industrial nations, and Israel's competitive position was enhanced.

The recession also stabilized prices. As Chart 3 shows, both consumer and wholesale prices stopped rising during mid-1966. From 1962 to 1966 consumer prices had risen 37 percent, or at an average annual rate of 7.4 percent. During the fourth quarter of 1966

Table 7.   UNIT LABOR COSTS IN ISRAEL
        AND DEVELOPED INDUSTRIAL COUNTRIES
                (1963 = 100)

	1964	1965	1966	1967	1968
Israel	108	119	139	137	134
Developed Industrial Countries	102	106	109	113	118
Relative Change in Israeli Unit Labor Costs	106	112	128	121	114

SOURCE: Bank of Israel, Annual Report 1969, p. 43.

Chart 3
PRICES

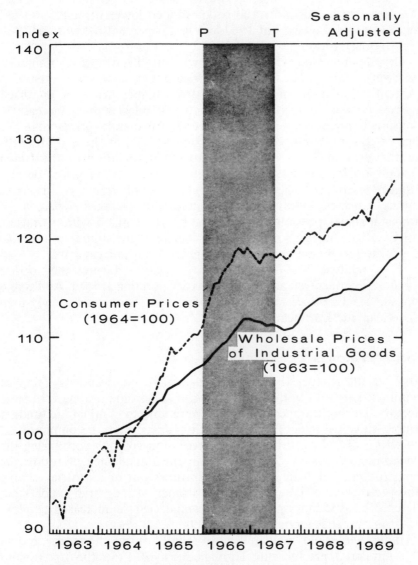

Note: P and T are Peak and Trough for the
entire economy.

Source: Central Bureau of Statistics,
Statistical Bulletin of Israel and
Statistical Abstract of Israel.

115

consumer prices reached a peak, and they edged slightly lower during 1967. This was the first time in Israel's history that consumer prices had shown no growth over a period as long as a year, a fairly rare achievement in most countries since the Great Depression. Wholesale prices of industrial goods slipped lower throughout 1967 and in the third quarter of 1967 averaged 1 percent below their 1966 fourth-quarter level.

Despite renewed economic growth in 1968, prices remained relatively stable. The consumer price index rose by a mere 2.1 percent (almost all of it resulting from higher prices of imported meat). Except for 1967, this was the smallest annual increase in consumer prices experienced in Israel. Wholesale prices rose 2.3 percent during 1968: the rise was concentrated in the early months of the year and was mainly due to the devaluation of the Israeli pound in November 1967. The relative stability of prices despite rising demand is explained by the underemployment of resources during most of 1968 – unemployment still averaged 6 percent – which made it possible to meet the higher demand without raising prices. Higher imports in 1968 also increased the supply of available goods, so less pressure was exerted against domestic capacity.

The relative stability of Israeli prices during the period 1967–1969 occurred as inflation was accelerating abroad. As Table 8 shows, Israel's prices for the first time were rising more slowly than American and European prices.

Industrial Structure

One result of the 1965–1969 business cycle was a shifting of employment both within the industrial sector and among economic sectors. During the recession firms were able to eliminate redundant labor, thus reducing their production costs, and the employment structure did not return to its pre-recession composition during the economic expansion. The decline in the importance of residential construction led to a shifting of resources out of industries serving this sector, while the increased importance of industrial exports and defense production among final demands led to increased employment in branches serving these markets.

Industrial employment fell more rapidly during the recession than did industrial production. Through most of 1966 the government remained surprisingly firm in the face of rising unemployment and refused to meet the demands of Histadrut and some elected officials as well as workers' demonstrations for crash programs to curb unemployment. In May Labor Minister Yigal Allon told the Knesset that the government would not back down from its restraint policy even if it meant "unavoidable temporary unemployment."[35] In fact,

Table 8. INCREASES IN CONSUMER PRICES IN ISRAEL
AND IN OTHER INDUSTRIAL COUNTRIES
(Percent Change)

	1962	1963	1964	1965	1966	1967	1968	1969
Israel	9.5	6.6	5.2	7.7	7.9	1.6	2.1	2.4
Other Industrial Countries*	3.6	3.5	3.4	3.9	4.2	3.0	3.6	4.9
Relative Change in Prices of Israel's Goods (1961 = 100)	105.7	108.9	110.7	114.8	119.0	117.4	115.6	113.0

*Data are unweighted averages of price changes in the United States, the United Kingdom, Japan, Germany, France, Holland, Belgium and Switzerland.

SOURCE: IMF, International Financial Statistics, Supplement, 1971.

117

he stated that the unemployment was necessary because many industries were not competitive in price and quality with those in foreign markets. "Unemployment," he said, "was the surest answer to increasing productivity and efficiency."[36] Histadrut, of course, objected to this idea that "a little unemployment is a good thing," but agreed not to interfere in cases where the dismissals were economically sound.[37] At least some of those laid off must have been redundant workers, since industrial production was able to regain and pass its previous peak level by the fourth quarter of 1967, while industrial employment remained 11.1 percent below its average 1965 level (see Chart 4). Although slack economic conditions forced Histadrut to accept layoffs of "permanent" workers[38], union regulations still hampered the most efficient layoff policies. For example, employers had to lay off workers with the least seniority in each area first rather than choosing to keep their most efficient workers. In large industrial countries like the United States, firms can evade such rules to some extent by closing an entire plant, but most Israeli firms have only one plant.

During the economic expansion the increased weight of exports and defense production among final demands produced a shifting of labor resources and output toward industry. Industrial employment continued to grow somewhat faster than total employment, reaching 26.2 percent of the total in 1969, whereas it had averaged 25.0 percent from 1961 to 1965. While official data on GNP at constant factor cost by industrial origin do not exist, estimates of the sectoral distribution of GNP by the Bank of Israel indicate that industry accounted for 27.9 percent of GNP in 1969 at constant factor prices, up from 25 percent in 1964.

During the 1965–1969 business cycle there was a definite change in the structure of industrial output. As Table 9 shows, sectors largely connected with construction, like nonmetallic minerals and wood products, as well as some consumer goods industries, like foods and textiles, declined as a proportion of industrial output. Conversely, those industries which experienced large export gains or which could supply defense equipment increased in importance. Thus the largest output gains were in basic metals, machinery, equipment, and electronics.

While industrial output gains connected with new defense requirements had no relationship to changes induced by the recession, it is difficult to separate the two effects, since virtually all of the "defense" industries were among those experiencing the fastest growth of exports. Exports of military equipment rose rapidly, reaching $50 million, 15 percent of industrial exports excluding diamonds, in 1970.[39] While lower costs and domestic demand in the economy enhanced the ability and interest of many industrial firms

118

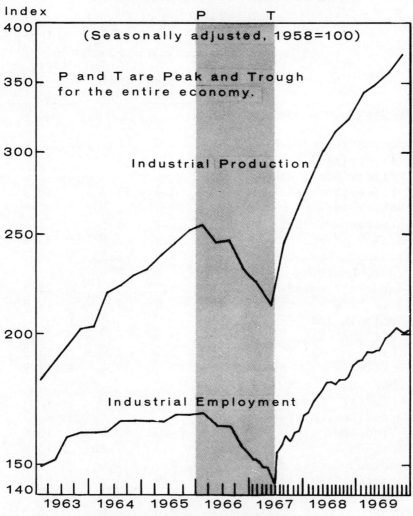

Chart 4

INDUSTRIAL PRODUCTION
AND INDUSTRIAL EMPLOYMENT

Index

P   T

400

(Seasonally adjusted, 1958=100)

350   P and T are Peak and Trough
for the entire economy.

300

Industrial Production

250

200

Industrial Employment

150

140

1963 1964 1965 1966 1967 1968 1969

Source: Central Bureau of Statistics
Monthly Bulletin of Statistics

Note: Industrial Production Index: 1963-1969
are quarterly data.

Industrial Employment Index: 1963-1966
are quarterly data; 1967-1969 are
monthly data.

Table 9. DISTRIBUTION OF REAL INDUSTRIAL OUTPUT
AND GROWTH OF EXPORTS
(Percent)

	Distribution of Output Year of Business Cycle			Export Growth (Annual Averages)
	Peak 1965	Trough 1967	Peak 1969	1965-1969
Industry				
Machinery (Incl. Electrical), Electronics, and Miscellaneous	7.0	8.9	12.6	50.9
Leather and Leather Products	4.0	1.7	1.5	38.4
Metal Products	7.1	6.2	6.8	36.1
Transport Equipment	4.4	6.9	8.2	27.3
Paper, Printing and Publishing	5.5	5.2	4.1	22.5
Basic Metals	2.0	2.4	2.7	17.7
Chemicals and Oil Refining	10.3	9.0	8.5	16.7
Mining	1.6	2.4	2.0	15.9
Textiles and Apparel	18.4	12.9	12.5	15.9
Rubber and Plastic Products	2.6	3.2	3.8	14.5
Food (Incl. Citrus Products)	21.6	24.0	19.8	13.8
Diamonds	3.4	7.3	7.7	13.3
Wood and Carpentry	6.9	4.9	5.4	5.6
Nonmetallic Minerals	5.3	4.9	4.5	-1.6
TOTAL	100.0	100.0	100.0	16.8

Note: 1965 was an atypical year for leather and
diamonds. In 1964, leather products accounted
for only 2.7 percent of output, while diamonds
accounted for 6.4 percent.

SOURCE: Bank of Israel, Annual Reports 1965 and 1969,
p. 267 and pp. 211 and 222 respectively.

in exports, higher defense orders may also have contributed to lower production costs in many of them. There may well have been economies of scale in producing some of these goods, and increased defense orders enabled some of these advantages to be realized. Given the structural problems of the Israeli economy, the limited size of its market made it impossible for many types of production to be maintained at economic levels of output. To the extent that the vast increase in defense spending since 1967 enabled some firms to attain economic levels of production, the effects of the recession in inducing exports by reducing costs have been overstated here.

Nevertheless, by decreasing domestic demand and lowering production costs, the recession set in motion economic forces which facilitated the growth of industry relative to other sectors, especially those capable of exporting. The recession was thus successful in shifting real resources into the areas desired by policymakers.

Between 1965 and 1969 the proportion of industrial output consumed by the public sector rose from 5 percent to 9 percent, while the proportion of industrial output channeled to exports rose from 23 percent to 30 percent.[40] As Table 10 shows, rough calculations based on the Bank of Israel's input-output tables indicate that the growth in exports was the major factor affecting the growth of industrial output during this period, with the exception of 1967.

The primary change in industrial output was from simpler stages of manufacture, like textiles and food processing, to more advanced

Table 10.   INCREASE IN INDUSTRIAL OUTPUT
STEMMING FROM CHANGES IN FINAL DEMANDS
(Percentages)

	1966	1967	1968	1969
Private Consumption	37	51	31	41
Public Consumption	63	67	10	5
Investment	-132	-64	15	22
Total Domestic Uses	-32	54	56	68
Exports	132	46	44	32
Total Uses	100	100	100	100

SOURCE: Bank of Israel, Annual Report 1969, p. 208.

121

stages, like producing capital goods. This kind of structural alteration is inherent in the development process and would be expected to occur in Israel simply as a result of its long-run economic development. Chart 5 and Table 11, however, show what appears to be an acceleration of this trend during the period under study. The fairly steady decline in the weight of primary processing industries from 1958 to 1963, and the steady increase in the weight of intermediate manufacturing and capital goods industries, was interrupted in 1964 and 1965. While the data are limited, the deviation from trend does appear consistent with other economic phenomena, such as the rising trade deficit, which indicate a diversion of resources toward consumption. In any case, the period following 1965 shows a marked acceleration of previous trends, most noticeably in the production of capital goods. The transfer of real resources from Type 1 industries to Type 3 industries in this latest period appears to have moved at a rate which had not been anticipated by long-run trends.

While Type 1 industries can be associated primarily with consumption, especially if mining and quarrying are removed (as shown on Chart 5 by Type 1 A), some consumer goods industries are also included among Type 3. Since the electrical machinery category includes many household appliances, one cannot conclude that the recession induced this transfer of resources simply by holding down consumption spending, although this was a factor. Nor was the decline in construction a sufficient condition, though it was probably a necessary one. At least part of the change in industrial structure was directly connected with more rapid gains in exports among Type 3 industries. As Table 9 indicates, for most Type 1 industries the growth rate of exports was below average, while all Type 3 industries had above-average growth rates. Moreover, industries supplying the construction sector declined in relative importance not only because of the slump in construction, but also because they had the lowest export growth rates in the industrial sector. The role of the government was again important in producing this shift to Type 3 industries: much of the increased production of transport and electronic equipment was stimulated by the French arms embargo and the increased efforts of the Israeli government to create a modern industrial defense establishment with its requisite science-based industries.

The distribution of industrial output by final demand changed during the recession and recovery periods. An increasing proportion of industrial output went to exports, which accounted for 30 percent of industrial output in 1969 compared to 23 percent in 1965.[41] While the historical trend has been for a growing proportion of industrial output to be allocated to exports, the growth during recent

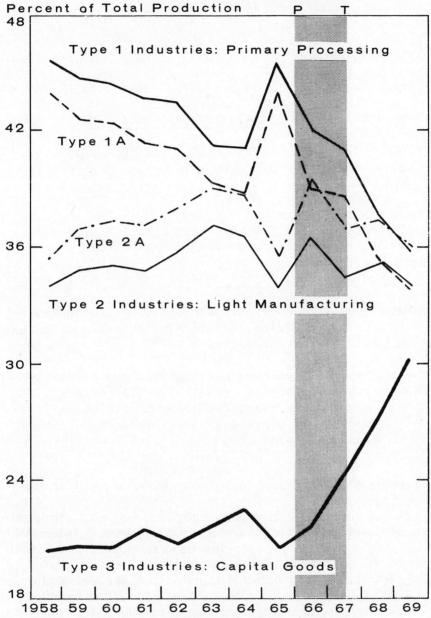

Chart 5

DISTRIBUTION OF REAL INDUSTRIAL OUTPUT
BY TYPE OF PRODUCTION

Percent of Total Production

Type 1 Industries: Primary Processing

Type 1A

Type 2A

Type 2 Industries: Light Manufacturing

Type 3 Industries: Capital Goods

Note: P and T are Peak and Trough for
the entire economy.

Source: Bank of Israel, Annual Reports.

123

Table 11.   DISTRIBUTION OF REAL INDUSTRIAL OUTPUT

	1958	1959	1960	1961	1962
Type 1 Industries	45.6	44.7	44.5	43.6	43.4
Type 2 Industries	33.9	34.7	35.1	34.8	35.8
Type 3 Industries	20.4	20.7	20.4	21.5	20.7
TOTAL	99.9	100.1	100.0	99.9	99.9
Type 1 A Industries Excluding Mining	44.0	42.5	42.3	41.3	41.1
Type 2 A Industries Including Mining	35.5	36.9	37.3	37.1	38.1

Note: Type 1 industries include mining and quarrying, food processing, textiles, clothing and leather and leather products.

Type 2 industries include wood and carpentry, rubber, plastics, chemicals, oil refining, nonmetallic minerals, diamond cutting and polishing, paper and paper products, printing and publishing.

years has been more rapid than during the boom period of 1962–1965. (See Chart 6.)

Part of the increase in exports since 1967 is due to a structural change involving trade with administered territories. Between 1948 and 1967 Israel did not have any trade relations with her Arab neighbors, but in 1969 sales to the administered areas accounted for 3.5 percent of its total industrial output.[42] Both the volume of trade and its composition indicate that at least some of the Israeli goods bought in the administered areas were for resale in Arab states. As the Bank of Israel's *Annual Report* discreetly noted, "Purchases by the inhabitants of the administered areas were not solely for the satisfaction of their own demand."[43]

1963	1964	1965	1966	1967	1968	1969
41.2	41.0	45.6	41.9	41.0	37.6	35.8
37.1	36.5	34.0	36.5	34.5	35.2	34.0
21.7	22.5	20.5	21.6	24.4	27.2	30.2
100.0	100.0	100.1	100.0	99.9	100.0	100.0
39.3	38.8	44.0	38.9	38.6	35.4	33.8
39.0	38.7	35.6	39.5	36.9	37.4	36.0

Type 3 industries include basic metals, metal products machinery, electrical equipment, electronics, transport equipment and miscellaneous.

SOURCE: Bank of Israel, Annual Reports 1959, p. 157; 1962, p. 220; 1963, p. 236; 1964, p. 267; 1965, p. 267; 1969, p. 211.

Of greater significance was the increased profitability of exports, as greater premiums, the 1967 devaluation, higher prices abroad, and the stability of domestic production costs led to a "steady uptrend in the profitability of these exports since 1966."[44] This was the major factor behind the diversification of industrial exports which occurred during the recovery. Diamonds, which for many years had accounted for most of the additional exports — 46 percent between 1963 and 1966 — have contributed a decreasing share since 1967 — only 27 percent in 1969.[45]

Chart 6

PROPORTION OF INDUSTRIAL OUTPUT
ALLOCATED TO EXPORTS

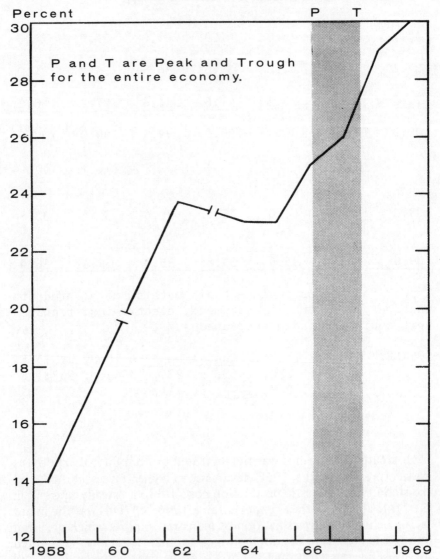

Percent

P and T are Peak and Trough
for the entire economy.

P   T

Note: About 2 and 3.5 percent of industrial
exports in 1968 and 1969, respectively,
went to administered areas.

Source: Bank of Israel, Annual Reports.

126

1.   Leonard G. Rosenberg, "Industrial Exports: Israel's Requirements for Self-Support," *Middle East Journal*, Spring, 1958, p. 164.

2.   *Ibid.*

3.   Eugene Van Cleef, "The Status of Israel – and a Look Ahead," *Middle East Journal*, Summer 1964, pp. 310 and 312.

4.   Moshe Yaacov Mandelbaum, "The Role of Development Loans Extended by the Israel Government in the Process of Industrialization 1956–1962" (Unpublished Ph. D. dissertation, Department of Economics, Vanderbilt University, January, 1968), p. 11.

5.   Nadav Halevi, "The Characteristics of Israel's Economic Growth," *Economic Development Issues: Greece, Israel, Taiwan, Thailand* (Supplementary Paper No. 25, Committee for Economic Development; New York: 1968), p. 118.

6.   Flora Davidov, "The Liberalization of Imports – February 1962 to May 1965," *Bulletin* (Bank of Israel, April 1966), p. 52

7.   I thank Dr. Arthur Bergman, President of the Maritime Bank and a former official in the Israeli Treasury, for pointing this out to me.

8.   See the following article by M. Tsur, Director-General, Ministry of Commerce and Industry: "Improving the Link Between Producer and Consumer," *Israel Economic Forum* (Ministry of Commerce and Industry, May 1961), pp. 20–21.

9.   If an investment is in a priority development area (Zone A), it receives an outright grant of 20 percent of its outlay for building and site development and one third of its outlay for machinery and equipment. If it is an industry which exports a high percentage of its output and locates in an area near the Negev or the Galilee (Zone B), it is given a grant for 15 percent of its outlay for building and site development and 25 percent of its outlay on machinery and equipment. If the industry locates in a densely populated section but exports a very high proportion of its outlay, it receives 10 percent and 20 percent respectively.

Beyond the outright grants, the Government assists the enterprise in obtaining loans of up to 55 percent of its investment in fixed assets in Zone A, up to 50 percent in Zone B and 45 percent in other areas. Moreover, the Government pays 50 percent of all outlays on research and development.

On taxes, an approved enterprise pays a corporate rate of only 25 percent during a five-year period. Dividends paid out of profits earned in this interval are exempt from further income tax. Other tax benefits include a forgiveness of two thirds of the property tax for five years, exemption from import duties on all materials needed to construct the plant and a depreciation schedule that is double the normal rate for five years. "Israel: The War-Peace Economy," *Dun's Review*, April, 1969, p. 67–68.

10.   Mandelbaum, *op. cit.*, p. 93.

11.   Central Bureau of Statistics, *Statistical Abstract of Israel 1968* (Jerusalem, 1968), p. 287. Many non-working housewives are also Histadrut members in order to obtain medical benefits of Kupat Holim.

12.   International Labor Office, *Report to the Government of Israel on Manpower Assessment and Planning* (Geneva, 1965), p. 29.

13.   This was the explanation given me by Jacob Arnon, Director of the Economic Planning Authority and Director-General of the Israeli Treasury.

14.   Pinchas Sapir, Minister of Finance, *Budget Address* as reported in *The Jerusalem Post*, November 19, 1965, p. 11.

15.   Horowitz told me this during a meeting we had in New York in October, 1969.

16.   Central Bureau of Statistics, *Monthly Bulletin of Statistics* (Jerusalem), May 1969, p. 37

17. *Ibid.*, p. 23.
18. Bank of Israel, *Annual Report 1966*, p. 331.
19. Central Bureau of Statistics, *Statistical Abstract of Israel 1967*, p. 405.
20. *Ibid.*
21. Haim Ben-Shahar and Marshall Sarnat, *New Issues and the Profitability of Investment in Common Stock, 1959–1964* (Research Paper No. 2; Jerusalem: The Hebrew University, Department of Business Administration, May 1966).
22. Bank of Israel, *Annual Report 1965*, p. 292.
23. Central Bureau of Statistics, *Monthly Bulletin...*, May 1969, p. 123.
24. *Ibid.*, p. 124.
25. Bank of Israel, *Annual Report 1968*, p. 71.
26. Economic Planning Authority, *Israel Economic Development, Past Progress and Plan for the Future* (Jerusalem, March 1968), p. 22.
27. Bank of Israel, *Annual Report 1966*, p. 101.
28. Arie Bregman, "The Influence of Changes in Investment on Product and Employment in Boom and Slump Periods in Israel (1965–1968)," *Bulletin* (Bank of Israel, July 1970), p. 8.
29. *Ibid.*
30. *Ibid.*, p. 9.
31. *Ibid.*, p. 10.
32. The nature of Israeli construction, with its preponderance of low rise concrete buildings, allows a large part of construction work to be done by relatively unskilled labor. This explains why large numbers of Arab workers in the post-1967 period were able to find employment in building.
33. Confidential source.
34. Central Bureau of Statistics, *Monthly Bulletin...*, several issues.
35. *The Jerusalem Post*, May 10, 1966, p. 1.
36. *Ibid.*
37. *The Jerusalem Post*, May 13, 1966, p. 10.
38. Permanent workers are those who have been employed for at least 90 days and thus cannot be dismissed without cause.
39. *The Jerusalem Post*, November 23, 1970, p. 9.
40. Bank of Israel, *Annual Report 1969*, p. 209.
41. Bank of Israel, *Annual Report 1969*, p. 209.
42. *Ibid.*
43. *Ibid.*
44. *Ibid.*, p. 217.
45. Bank of Israel, *Annual Reports 1968* and *1969*, p. 50–51, and p. 38, respectively.

CHAPTER VII

PRIVATE CONSUMPTION
AND AN INCOMES POLICY

One statement from the report of Israel's Economic Planning Authority clearly indicates that the government was aware that the rapid rise in living standards was the decisive factor in maintaining the large import surplus:

> The rise in the purchasing power of the growing population, on top of the protection given to local production, encouraged investments aimed at satisfying local private consumption. Since the relative ease with which products could be sold on the domestic market hindered the rise in exports, the economy paid for the rise in private consumption by foregoing the possibility of allocating investments to the production of export commodities, and thus liberating the economy from its dependence on capital imports.[1]

When in 1964 it appeared that the capital inflows necessary for the import surplus would not continue to be available, it was clear that the growth of consumption would have to be reduced. In October 1965 Prime Minister Eshkol stressed that the newly elected government would give high priority to reducing private consumption below the 6 percent real per capita annual increase of recent years. He called on the high-income groups to set an example by reducing their consumption and increasing their saving.[2]

Between 1950 and 1965 real private consumption rose fivefold, while real private consumption per capita doubled. During 1960–1965 real consumption continued to increase at an average annual rate of 10 percent, and per capita real consumption by 6 percent. In international terms, this was an extremely high rate of growth: by 1965 the average level of private consumption expenditure in Israel was similar to that of developed countries like Norway and Holland.[3]

The growth of private consumption reflected primarily the substantial increase in private incomes. Disposable income from domestic sources rose by 9.5 percent each year from 1950 to 1966, and private transfers from abroad added another 12 percent during 1955–1964. Wage gains have been severely inflationary: Evans' econometric equations showed that at a 4 percent unemployment rate wages would rise by 14.3 percent per year[4], which agrees very closely with the actual annual increase during the sample period 1952–1965, 14.0 percent. Evans found that a lagged price change term in the wage rate equations was quite important, largely because of the cost-of-living clauses which affect virtually all wage earners.

The upward push on wages and prices, coupled with redistribution away from the government and toward wage-earners, leads to a rise in real purchasing power which is financed through increases in relatively cheaper imports, particularly capital imports. This in turn pushes the economy closer and closer to zero unemployment and more and more inflation, if no move toward definite fiscal policy is taken.[5]

The Government's Incomes Policies and Consumption: 1964–1969

The government's wage agreements with public employees in 1964 and 1965 raised average hourly wages in the public sector by 24 percent in 1965 and increased inflationary pressures throughout the economy.[6] Having itself capitulated to a very large wage increase in the public sector, the government was not in a very strong position for dictating to Histadrut in the 1966 wage negotiations. Nevertheless, it did try to induce some moderation in private wage demands by limiting increases in basic wages to increases in productivity. At Histadrut's convention in January 1966, Finance Minister Pinchas Sapir warned that the country faced severe economic conditions. Stable prices, he argued, were essential for the well-being of the country, and they depended on wage restraint. He urged a wage freeze for white-collar workers and wage increases of not more than 5 percent for production workers.[7]

The unions, however, negotiated contracts based on the inflationary conditions of the previous years. The new contracts called for gains of 5 to 10 percent for 1966, a further 5 percent boost in 1967, and cost-of-living adjustments every six months. These wage increases exceeded the expected rise in productivity — in January 1966 the cost-of-living adjustment alone added 7 percent more to the wage bill — and would therefore exert new pressure on prices and costs in 1966. Since the gains were nevertheless lower than those granted public employees in 1965, Histadrut had a difficult time persuading its members to accept the agreement. Several large groups of workers, most notably those in the ports, protested with long strikes.

The dual role of Histadrut as union and national institution was clearly evident in its struggle with both the government and the workers over the appropriate wage increase. The secretary-general of

Histadrut warned the workers that "the abyss of runaway inflation has opened before us." He demanded to know whether they wanted Histadrut "to be popular for a few hours, or to remain a responsible body dedicated to preserve the true interests of the workers and the state?"[8]

While Histadrut was battling the workers, the government announced new tax increases, amounting to an 8.5 percent rise in overall tax rates, to pay for the higher wages granted civil servants. Income tax rates were raised by 1.5 – 2.5 percent, and company taxes 1.5 percent. A host of indirect taxes were also increased to raise IL 260 million, exactly the expected increase in the government's wage bill.[9]

There was considerable dissatisfaction among economists with these policies. Don Patinkin, the country's leading economist, publicly chastized the government for not cutting expenditures and for not having taken a stronger stand on union wage restraint. Soon after the new union contracts went into effect, the faculty of the Hebrew University, the nation's leading university, attempted to mobilize public support for wage restraint by announcing it would forego the retroactive payment of its higher wages if other groups would follow and if the government would reduce the indirect tax levies and cut expenditures further.[10] A few days later the faculties of the Weizmann Institute, the nation's leading scientific research center, and Technion, its great technical university, expressed their support of this proposal. Other professional groups soon followed. The Defense Industries senior staff offered to forego 5 percent of their gross wages.[11] Not to be outdone, the President, Cabinet, State Comptroller, and Knesset members waived their salary increases, too.

The government also announced further restrictive measures, including the dismissal of 500 civil servants and a further cut of IL 100 million in expenditures. (The development budget had previously been cut by IL 250 million.) Prime Minister Eshkol stated that these further steps would allow the budget to achieve an IL 50 million surplus. He also removed some of the higher indirect taxes affecting the poor and added an additional IL 25 million subsidy to hold down food prices.

During February and March 1966 offers of voluntary wage cuts from private individuals continued. Prime Minister Eshkol, in a radio broadcast, called on the workers to respect the public's fear of a wage-induced inflationary spiral and to reduce the wage increases in their new contracts. A Histadrut committee was set up to "organize" the voluntary wage cut offers which were "inundating" the Prime Minister's office and to determine how the money would be used.[12]

Governor Horowitz of the Bank of Israel was quite heartened by the public's response: "I do not know any other country where thousands of people have surrendered a part of their wages of their own free will in time of peace."[13] He added that efforts to restrain living standards to those commensurate with Israel's productive capacity were absolutely necessary since "the world does not owe us a living."[14] Although the unions never renegotiated their contracts, by the movement's peak in March, about 100,000 persons, 11 percent of the employed civilian labor force, had voluntarily waived part of their wage increases.[15]

After March attention shifted to forcing the unions to give up the July cost-of-living increases. Finance Minister Sapir warned that an additional allowance payment would cause "untold damage to the economy."[16] Through the spring the government continued the pressure on Histadrut to forego the adjustment, even after the left-wing Mapam party members of the government coalition attacked this proposal as unfair to the workers. In June, confronted with rapidly rising unemployment, Histadrut agreed to waive the July payment but maintained its adherence to the principle of linking wages to prices. The June 1966 agreement provided that the allowance would be increased in the following January if prices had by then risen by more than 3 percent since the last increase and again in July 1967 only if prices had risen by more than 5 percent during the preceding six months. (Previously, an increase had been due in January 1967 and again in July if prices had risen by 3 percent.) The new system did not apply to employees who earned less than IL 400 per month, who also obtained a 5 percent increase in July 1966. The semi-annual revision of their allowance was to continue as in the past. The increased payments, however, were not to be paid by the employers, as previously, but were to be financed by the government through the National Insurance Institute, Israel's Social Security Administration. With unemployment at 8.4 percent in the third quarter and rising rapidly, Histadrut agreed to reduce the allowance to only half of the rise in the cost-of-living index in 1967 and 1968. This decision did not apply to the increased allowance paid by the National Insurance Institute to low-wage employees.

The deteriorating employment situation also affected wage rates. Wage drift, which had been so common during the preceding boom, disappeared. Sharply rising unemployment even forced reductions in union wage rates at the plant level. Employees, especially in the smaller concerns, were forced to accept wages lower than those specified in the national contracts in order to keep their jobs.

Histadrut also decided that the wage increases to be negotiated in 1968 would be kept in line with productivity gains, as measured for each industrial branch by the Productivity Institute. Salaries in the service sector were to be increased by the same amount as the average productivity in the industrial sector. The government policy also specified that part of the increased output should be used to strengthen the financial position of the enterprises and to reward capital.

In March 1967, after negotiations with the Manufacturers Association and the government, Histadrut again decided to waive any cost-of-living adjustment because of high unemployment. In compensation for this freeze, the government again agreed that the National Insurance Institute should pay the cost-of-living grants to those with low incomes. Thus the restrictive fiscal and monetary policies were able to reduce the coefficients of wage adjustment, as Michaely had predicted they would.[17]

The other elements of the economic policy designed to support the incomes policy remained largely unchanged. The government committed itself not to increase taxes further, although deductible business expenses were to be reduced and the capital gains tax increased from 25 percent to 30 percent. The government also agreed not to reduce price subsidies any further and not to relax price surveillance by the Price Headquarters.

To combat unemployment, the government set up an Employment Headquarters and declared its readiness to examine recommendations to initiate unemployment insurance legislation. Despite rising unemployment, however, the government also declared its intention to halt the growth of the civil service. The Jewish Agency, in line with this policy, announced that it was reducing its staff by 25 percent and that it would halve the number of its departments. A wage freeze was also imposed in the public service. These savings were designed to help the government balance the budget, despite increased expenditures on export incentives.

Rising unemployment had accomplished what the previous use of an incomes policy alone had failed to do in the years 1962–1965. The wage/price spiral, which had been an inherent part of the Israeli economic climate, was broken by high unemployment, making labor less insistent on a complete adjustment for higher prices. High unemployment also ended wage drift, which had substantially added to cost pressures in previous years.

The slowdown in economic activity which began in late 1965 was reflected during the second half of 1965 in a lessening of income gains from domestic economic activities at the same time that personal restitution payments dropped 16 percent in 1965 from their previous year's level. Consumer spending also slowed from the 11 percent average annual gain during the 1961–1964 period to an 8 percent increase. All of the decline in consumer spending was concentrated in purchases of durable goods, which rose only 5 percent in 1965 after climbing 24 percent in 1964. Purchases of consumer durables were also affected by the end of the residential building boom, which lowered purchases of household equipment, and by the imposition of higher import taxes on autos in late 1964, which led to a 17 percent drop in auto purchases in 1965.

Despite the large wage gains obtained in the new wage agreements in 1966, income fell much more rapidly in 1966, as unemployment rose from 3.3 percent of the labor force in the first half of 1965 to 10.3 percent in the fourth quarter of 1966. Since Israel had no unemployment compensation insurance until early 1967, that automatic stabilizer was not available to buttress incomes as unemployment rose.[18] Real disposable income per capita fell 3.1 percent in 1966. Personal restitution receipts also slipped lower. The change in consumer purchases of durable goods was quite dramatic: by the fourth quarter of 1966 such purchases were only 75 percent of their level in the fourth quarter of 1965. These cutbacks continued as the recession deepened during the first half of 1967, and real consumption per capita fell 2 percent in 1967.

Imports for private consumption accounted for about 30 percent of total imports during the 1960's.[19] Thus the 3.6 percent decline in total real consumption expenditures between 1965 and the first quarter of 1967 accounted for a 1.08 percent decline in total imports. However, imports of consumer durables, which had doubled between 1962 and 1964, fell much more strikingly, dropping to two-thirds of their 1964 level in the first half of 1967. The mild decline in disposable income thus had an important effect in holding down imports. (Total imports of goods and services at constant 1964 prices rose 2.2 percent from the fourth quarter of 1965 to the first half of 1967.)

In the period immediately after the Six-Day War, the government was able to capitalize on its strengthened political position and the widespread feelings of national unity to persuade Histadrut to agree to a wage-freeze in 1968 and 1969. The cost-of-living allowance was to be granted only if the price index had risen by more than 3 percent during the previous year. This agreement added a large element of cost stability to the economy during the expansion.

Although the union was partly forced by the government, it did in fact accept the goal of expanding exports. An IMF delegation to Israel in January 1968 was quite impressed with the reasonableness of Histadrut leaders.

> For their part, the representatives of the Histadrut with whom the staff team had talks showed a great awareness of the problems that excessive wage increases and overfull employment can bring. They stated that it was their intention over the long run to base the increase in total wage payments per worker on the increase in

134

productivity in the economy so as to safeguard the international competitiveness of Israel production and the sustained growth of the economy.[20]

It was clear, however, that unless demand pressures were restrained so that no shortage of labor would develop, the Federation, under pressure from its own members, would not be able to pursue its declared policy. The government, as part of the package, agreed not to raise tax rates. While prices were not officially frozen, the agreement to extend the wage freeze into 1969 was dependent upon the performance of prices in 1968. The increase in prices that occurred as a result of the devaluation in November 1967 reduced the leeway for additional increases from purely internal developments. The prospects for maintaining wage and price stability after the 1969 agreement ended were also endangered by the large public sector deficits. By 1969 these deficits had begun to create excessive demands on Israel's resources.

The importance of restraining incomes became abundantly clear during the economic recovery. Despite the wage freeze, per capita real disposable income rose 13.8 percent in 1968 because of the decline in unemployment and the higher IL value of capital transfers from abroad.[21] As a result, real private consumption expenditures rose 11.8 percent; the rate on a per capita basis, 8.2 percent[22], exceeded even that for the period 1960–1965, when it had averaged 6 percent.[23] Real purchases of consumer durable goods soared 75.6 percent over their 1967 level to a new peak 31.7 percent higher than their previous 1965 peak level. In 1969 real disposable private income on a per capita basis rose again by a rapid 7.5 percent and real per capita consumption expenditures gained 9 percent.[24] Again, higher spending most noticeably affected purchases of consumer durables, which soared another 40 percent in real terms in 1969.[25] The accelerated rise in consumption is explained by the renewed growth in income and the standstill in consumption during the recession.

While imports of consumer goods rose 46 percent in 1968 and 26 percent in 1969, imports of consumer durables more than doubled in 1968 and climbed 59 percent more in 1969 as Israelis spent significant parts of their higher incomes on imported cars and television sets. National television began in the second quarter of 1968, and by 1970 half of all Israeli families owned television sets, up from 30 percent in 1969 and 10.5 percent in 1968.[26] In addition to imports of finished goods, many imports are used for the domestic manufacture of consumer goods. The weight of imports for private consumption in total imports averaged 27.6 percent during 1968 and 1969[27] and thus markedly affected the trade balance. Part of the explanation of why higher consumer spending did not raise domestic prices is also found in this marked worsening of the balance of trade.

The Israeli government has been severely criticized by both its own and foreign economists for allowing such rapid growth in private incomes and consumption. With the exception of a 10 percent income tax surcharge imposed immediately after the Six-Day War and the floating of a defense loan, the government did not raise taxes on incomes. Because Israel was in a state of war throughout this period, the public sector required a larger share of total resources and other uses therefore had to be reduced. In a country still needing major investments and with a perfectly adequate standard of living, it would have been appropriate to restrain consumption by increasing taxation. The Israeli government's failure to use this instrument not only enlarged the trade deficit unnecessarily by increasing imports, but also led to a diversion of exportable goods back to the home market.

The Effectiveness of Israel's Incomes Policy

The efficacy of the incomes policy can be tested by comparing the actual wage increases with what they might have been during and after a recession in the absence of an incomes policy. By estimating the relationship between wage changes and changes in unemployment rates and prices from 1957 to 1965, we can forecast expected wage increases in the years 1966 to 1969 if there had been no incomes policy. These forecasted wage changes are compared with actual wage gains in Table 1. Any significant differences between the two values could then be attributed to wage restraint induced by the incomes policy.

This test is based on the work of Professors Phillips and Lipsey[28], who demonstrated that a nonlinear inverse relationship exists between the level of unemployment and the rate of change of money wage rates. Lipsey included the rate of change of the level of unemployment and the rate of change in the cost of living in addition to the unemployment rate in his relationship, variables which Phillips had suggested but had not combined explicitly into his equation.

The index of average hourly wage rates taken from the Bank of Israel's *Annual Reports* provided a measure of the rate of change of money wage rates ($\dot{W}$). For the unemployment rate (U), the official figures from the Central Bureau of Statistics manpower surveys were used. The rate of change in the consumer price index (P) was used as the indicator of the price variable. By taking the absolute changes in the unemployment rate and prices as $(U_t - U_{t-1})$ and $(P_t - P_{t-1})$, a six-months' lag was in effect introduced into those variables.

The form of the estimated relationship was

$$\log \dot{W}_t = a + b \log U_t + c \log \dot{P}_t$$

or $W_t = \dfrac{a}{U_t{}^{|b|}} \, (\dot{P}_t{}^{c})$, with b expected to be negative

The estimated relationship was

$$\log \dot{W}_t = .98 - .62 \, U_t + .48 \, \dot{P}_t$$

with t ratios (2.05) (3.76)

$$R^2 = 0.87 \qquad \text{S.E.} = 0.083 \qquad \text{D.W.} = 1.85.$$

When, on the basis of a one-tail test with six degrees of freedom, the regression coefficients were tested for significance, U_t was found to be significant at the 5 percent level and $\dot{P}_t$ at the 1 percent level. The

Table 1.   ESTIMATED AND ACTUAL MONEY WAGE
RATE INCREASES IN ISRAEL, 1957–1969
(Percent Change)

	Actual	Estimated**
1957	8.2	7.6
1958	5.3	6.7
1959	4.9	4.0
1960	4.5	5.6
1961	10.0	11.2
1962	12.3	13.5
1963	10.7	11.5
1964	11.4	10.5
1965	18.0	12.2
1966*	19.8	7.5
1967*	3.0	4.9
1968*	0.3	4.2
1969*	3.2	7.2

*These years were not included in the data used to estimate the regression equation.

**The percentage equivalent of the standard error for the log equation is 0.68.

coefficient of multiple correlation for this equation was $R^2 = .87$ and adjusted for degrees of freedom was $R^2 = .82$. The Durbin-Watson coefficient for the equation was 1.85.

Using the actual and estimated rates of change of money wage rates between 1957 and 1969, shown in Table 1, the mathematical analysis indicates that in 1966 the actual rate of change of money wage rates was far higher than would have been expected on the basis of economic conditions. The recession did not have an immediate impact on wages because new wage agreements, negotiated in late 1965, went into effect in early 1966. As a result, wages including cost-of-living payments rose 20 percent during 1966, despite rising unemployment and official calls for wage restraint. All of the rise in wages, however, occurred during the first half of the year, primarily during the first three months of 1966.

A comparison of the actual and estimated rates of change of money wage rates for 1967–1969 indicates that the actual rate lies significantly below the predicted rate, particularly during the latter two years, when a freeze was in effect. The t values indicate that the differences between the actual and estimated rates were significant at the 1 percent level for each year between 1967 and 1969. Thus it is possible to state with an acceptable degree of confidence that the "compulsory" restraint of wages during the last three years of this period had an effect over and above the effects of the deflationary measures.

On the basis of these figures, the incomes policy, when it was fighting a cost-push inflation during the closing months of a recession and during the ensuing economic recovery, must be regarded as a success. Part of its success during the economic expansion must, of course, be attributed to the powerful political position enjoyed by the government and the unifying national feeling which followed the Six-Day War. As pointed out previously, however, restraining wage increases was not a sufficiently restrictive incomes policy since declining unemployment and large foreign capital transfers still allowed rapid increases in real incomes and consumption.

Annual figures may to some extent understate the effects of deflationary measures. Thus large wage increases went into effect in the first quarter of 1966, when the unemployment rate was only 4.6 percent, substantially below the yearly average level of 7.4 percent, and the government's call for wage restraint went unheeded. During the second half of the year wages were stable as the combination of rising unemployment and government demands led to nonpayment of the cost-of-living allowance. Similarly, as the unemployment rate edged down to 4.5 percent in the latter half of 1969, wages, which had been stable in the opening months of the year, began to rise. Even with these reservations, the regression analysis supports the

138

conclusion that the incomes policy was an effective supplement to the deflationary measures.

1.   Economic Planning Authority, *Israel Economic Development, Past Progress and Plan for the Future* (Jerusalem, March 1968), p. 23.
2.   *The Jerusalem Post*, October 24, 1965, p. 1.
3.   International Monetary Fund, *International Financial Statistics* (Washington, D.C., 1966). Private consumption per capita in 1965 in Israel was $935; in Norway, $1,037; and in Holland, $898. See country pages.
4.   Michael K. Evans, *An Econometric Model of Part of the Israeli Economy* (Discussion Paper No. 86; Philadelphia: University of Pennsylvania), p. 20.
5.   *Ibid.*, p. 58.
6.   See page 33 for a more detailed account of the wage agreements.
7.   Talk to Histadrut convention reported in *The Jerusalem Post*, January 6, 1966, p. 1.
8.   Speech quoted in *The Jerusalem Post* February 15, 1966, p. 7.
9.   *The Jerusalem Post*, February 15, 1966, p. 7.
10.   The University faculties, like other public employees, had received a large readjustment of salary scales in the summer of 1965 which was retroactive to April, 1964.
11.   *The Jerusalem Post*, February 17, 1966, p. 1.
12.   *The Jerusalem Post*, February 28, 1966, p. 6; March 1, 1966, p. 6; March 2, 1966, p. 8.
13.   *The Jerusalem Post*, February 27, 1966, p. 8.
14.   *Ibid.*
15.   *The Jerusalem Post*, March 16, 1966, p. 8.
16.   *The Jerusalem Post*, April 17, 1966, p. 8.
17.   Michael Michaely, "Devaluation, Cost Inflation and the Supply of Exports," *Economia Internazionale*, IX (February, 1956).
18.   Unemployment insurance was opposed by the left-wing political parties, who felt it was the Government's job to provide jobs for all instead of payments for not working. During 1966, Yigal Allon, Minister of Labor, voiced this view on numerous occasions. See *The Jerusalem Post*, May 10, 1966, p. 1.
19.   Bank of Israel, *Annual Report 1968*, p. 87.
20.   Confidential source.
21.   Bank of Israel, *Annual Report 1969*, p. 18. Private transfers from abroad, which had averaged about IL 800 million annually in the period 1963–1967, jumped to IL 1242 in 1968 and to IL 1398 in 1969.
22.   Bank of Israel, *Annual Report 1968*, p. 74.
23.   *Ibid.*, p. 75.
24.   Bank of Israel, *Annual Report 1969*, pp. 19 and 56.
25.   *Ibid.*, p. 67.
26.   *The Jerusalem Post*, January 11, 1971, p. 14 and Bank of Israel, *Annual Report 1969*, p. 69.
27.   Bank of Israel, *Annual Report 1969*, p. 60.
28.   A.W. Phillips, "The Relation Between Unemployment and the Rate of Change of Money Wage Rates in the United Kingdom, 1861–1957," *Economica*, NSXXV, 1958 and R.G. Lipsey, "The Relation Between Unemployment and the Rate of Change of Money Wage Rates in the United Kingdom, 1862–1957: A Further Analysis," *Economica*, NSXXVII, 1960.

CHAPTER VIII

CONCLUSION: POLICY ALTERNATIVES

It is clear from the preceding analysis of the Israeli experience that the recession did create forces which led to a decline in the import surplus. This resulted not only from a decline in imports but also from a more rapid expansion of industrial exports. But the recession was a very costly policy in terms of lost output and unemployment. If real GNP had continued to grow in the 1965 to 1967 period at the 10.8 percent growth rate of the 1961 to 1964 period, it would have been IL 1.9 billion or 19 percent higher in 1967 than it actually was.[1] Unemployment would not have climbed to 12.4 percent of the labor force, as it did in 1967. (GNP could have continued growing, of course, only if capital inflows had continued at high enough levels to allow rapid development and a growing import surplus.) The benefit obtained from this sacrifice of real output was a drop in the import surplus: if the import surplus had continued to grow at its 1961–1964 rate of 13.3 percent, it would have been IL 1.1 billion higher in 1967 than the actual surplus, or IL 1.6 billion higher than the actual surplus would have been if defense imports in 1967 had remained at their 1966 level.[2]

One can compare benefits with costs by dividing the loss in real GNP by the decline in the import surplus to arrive at an exchange rate of domestic output for dollars saved. Without adjusting for higher defense imports, the decline in the import surplus cost $1 = IL 1.7 not a high rate, compared to the official exchange rate during this period of $1 = IL 3.0. If defense imports were held constant at their 1966 level, the exchange would be an even more reasonable $1 = IL 1.19.

The government's decision to employ restrictive monetary and fiscal policies has been attacked by Israeli economists, who have argued that alternative policies were available which would not have entailed such a large sacrifice in real output. Halevi, Barkai, Kleiman, Beham, and others argue that the government aimed its policies at curbing excess aggregate demand while inflationary pressures were actually being generated by the cost-push of wage claims. While agreeing that measures which resulted in higher unemployment were wasteful, they proposed some strikingly different alternatives.

140

Barkai and Kleiman believe that the government in late 1965 or early 1966 should have devalued from $1 = IL 3 to $1 = IL 5. Since the goal of the slowdown policy was to shift resources into exports, they argue that the most effective means of accomplishing this was to change relative prices in a way that made exports more profitable. Changing the price of exports directly through a devaluation would have been more efficient than using unemployment to lower prices. A devaluation, by raising the price of imports, would also have cut consumer purchasing power and decrease the demand for imports, further helping the trade balance.

It is important to note that a devaluation in early 1966 might have furthered the government's goals only if the economy were already in a recession. In early 1966 no one in Isreal realized that the economy had already slowed down, since only the construction sector had become sluggish (and even there activity was still quite high because of work on buildings started earlier). A delegation of Israeli economists visited the Bank of Israel and voiced their support for restrictive monetary policies[3], and economists at the Hebrew University were still calling on the government to cut the budget further. By mid-1966 enough data had become available to indicate that the economy was in a recession, and a devaluation might have been opportune. In June the staff of the Bank of Israel joined the academic economists in arguing for one.[4]

According to Eliezer Sheffer, Director of Research at the Bank of Israel, the government rejected the devaluation proposal solely for political reasons. Devaluations are usually seen by politicians as an indictment of their past policies, as an admission of failure. In addition, given Israel's already high taxes, the government may have been wary of substantially increasing the domestic currency cost of servicing Israel's large foreign debt. On purely political grounds, the government may also have been concerned about increasing the financial power of the Jewish Agency in relation to that of the government. A devaluation would increase the domestic currency value of contributions to the Jewish Agency without increasing their dollar volume. Nevertheless, the Jewish Agency would be able to command additional domestic resources.

While devaluations are always unpopular with the public, an Israeli devaluation might lead to higher consumption spending and to a redistribution of income by increasing the domestic currency value of German restitution payments to individuals. With the failure of the 1962 devaluation still fresh in everyone's mind, arguments that economic conditions were sufficiently different to produce a successful devaluation were viewed skeptically. Instead, the government chose in late 1966 to increase export subsidies. This added to the drain on the budget, but its price effects were so small, compared

141

to the proposed devaluation to $1 = IL 5$, that it had a much smaller impact on producers' decisions.

Although the government may have missed an opportunity by not devaluing in the second half of 1966, when the unemployment rate was climbing above 6 percent, an earlier devaluation would have caused wages, which are tied to the cost-of-living index, to jump sharply at the time. Barkai's and Kleiman's argument implicitly assumes that with the unemployment rate at a mere 4 percent, as it was in early 1966, and with the major wage negotiations in process, labor would have allowed its real income to be cut drastically. At the very least, Histadrut would not have given up its cost-of-living adjustment in June 1966 to offset the sharp rise in prices which would have occurred. While Barkai and Kleiman would have had the devaluation offset the higher wages negotiated in the 1966 contracts, it is very likely that such a sharp devaluation, coming just after the contracts had been signed, would have led to the widespread abrogation of the contracts and wildcat strikes to obtain new ones.

Barkai's and Kleiman's counter-argument that more income was actually lost through higher unemployment than would have occurred through a devaluation – and without the inefficiencies of lost output – is really beside the point. In early 1966, with unemployment still low, labor did not know and would not have believed that a severe recession was in the offing. Nor could the economists foresee the depths of the 1966–1967 recession. Under these circumstances no powerful labor union would agree to a sharp cut in real wages, and a devaluation would soon have had little effect even on relative prices.

If the Bank of Israel did not validate the higher wage and price level stimulated by the devaluation by increasing the money supply, then the higher unemployment which Barkai and Kleiman were trying to avoid would have occurred in any case. The only feasible solution was to allow unemployment to rise to levels where labor was worried enough about its own position that it would not have demanded an immediate adjustment of wages to prices. This occurred in the second half of 1966, and a devaluation at that time would have aided the adjustment process.

One could argue, of course, that Histadrut gave up the cost-of-living adjustment not only because unemployment was so high but also because prices were rising so slowly. If the government had effected a large rise in prices through a sharp devaluation, it is quite conceivable that labor would have continued to insist on payment of the allowance. Because of the economic strength of Histadrut and the pervasiveness of cost-of-living adjustments, a devaluation might have been a mistake at any time other than the months immediately following the June war, when the government could assert unusual pressures on the Histadrut and avoid the wage increases which might well have come in 1966 despite the slack in the economy.

Halevi, seeking to fight the wage-push inflation through a direct confrontation of the government with labor, proposed that the government announce firm plans to raise personal income tax rates to offset wage increases granted in the new contracts. At first glance, this appears to be a clever way to remove any incentive to bargain for higher wages. Management could effectively argue that higher wages would only raise costs and therefore prices without actually increasing the take-home pay of workers. Such a proposal could be contemplated only in a country like Israel, where one giant union negotiates one basic wage increase for most of the labor force. Even there, however, it would create problems.

Wages including the cost-of-living adjustment rose about 20 percent in 1966, so if the average tax rate were 25 percent, it would have had to have been raised 17 percentage points, or 43 percent, to an average tax rate of 42 percent for after-tax income to remain unchanged. One need only point to the problems economists faced in the United States Congress in 1967, when they tried to obtain a 10 percent surcharge on the income tax, or a rise of 1 percent in the average rate, to doubt whether the Knesset would have felt it politically feasible to raise the average tax rate by the required amount.

Aside from the political problems Halevi's plan would have faced, there is the question of what the government would have done with the higher revenue. If it did not spend a substantial portion of it, the deflationary effects of the tax on top of the higher costs facing producers would have pushed the economy into a very severe recession. If the government did spend its higher receipts in order to maintain aggregate demand, the increased taxes would then lead neither to lower wage costs nor to higher exports.

Halevi's plan would work only if it frightened labor into accepting a wage freeze. While it is conceivable that it would have had this effect, it is not likely that all groups would have accepted it. With unemployment low, certain groups, such as the port workers, might have gone on strike. Piecemeal wage increases would have made the tax increase program exceedingly more difficult to administer, since individual gains resulting from basic wage increases would have to be separated from those resulting from new jobs or job promotions. As pointed out previously, the feasibility of this proposal was founded on the central wage adjustment process of Histadrut. With different groups of various sizes obtaining different rates of wage increases, it would have been virtually impossible to administer a tax increase of the kind proposed by Halevi. And if enough individual groups obtained wage increases, then the government would again have been faced either with spending its higher tax revenues to support aggregate demand or with precipitating a deflation. On examination, neither Halevi's nor Barkai's alternative policies would have allowed the government to escape from the "inefficient" but inevitable use of higher unemployment as a means of fighting inflation.

A recession was the only viable policy alternative actually available, and it successfully implemented both the short- and long-range policy goals of the Israeli government. The short-term goal was to decrease as quickly as possible the import surplus. An immediate cut in imports was necessitated by the imminent decline in unilateral capital transfers. A sure way of accomplishing this short-term goal was to slow the rate of economic growth, thus decreasing the need for industrial inputs and cutting the level of consumer spending. In addition, the recession furthered the long-run goals of moving resources into industries producing for export. This was accomplished by shifting real resources out of residential construction and other domestic-oriented industries. By lowering relative wage costs, the recession also raised the profitability of exports. This restructuring of the Israeli economy allowed Israel to renew rapid growth with an economic structure more aligned to its development needs.

1. All comparisons are made between GNP and the import surplus in constant 1964 prices.
2. The actual import surplus in 1967 was IL 1750 million, in 1964 prices. If defense imports had remained at their 1966 level, the import surplus would have been IL 1250 million in 1967.
3. Eliezer Sheffer, Director of Research of the Bank of Israel, described this meeting to me.
4. The support of the Bank of Israel Research Staff for a devaluation was not, however, made known publicly.

144

BIBLIOGRAPHY

Books and Pamphlets

Akzin, Benjamin, and Dror, Yehezekel. *Israel, High-Pressure Planning*. Syracuse, New York: Syracuse University Press, 1966.

Bahral, Uri. *The Effect of Mass Immigration on Wages in Israel*. Jerusalem: The Falk Project for Economic Research in Israel, May, 1965.

Barkai, Haim. "The Public, Histadrut and Private Sectors in the Israeli Economy," *Sixth Report 1961–1963*. Jerusalem: The Falk Project for Economic Research in Israel, 1964.

Beham, Miriam. *Monetary Aspects of the 1962 Devaluation*. Jerusalem: The Maurice Falk Institute for Economic Research in Israel, October, 1968.

Ben-Shahar, Haim, and Sarnat, Marshall. *New Issues and the Profitability of Investment in Common Stock*. Research Paper No. 2. Jerusalem: Hebrew University, May, 1966.

Bruno, Michael. *Interdependence, Resource Use and Structural Changes in Israel*. Research Department Special Studies No. 2. Jerusalem: Bank of Israel, 1962.

Burns, Arthur F., and Mitchell, Wesley C. *Measuring Business Cycles*. New York: National Bureau of Economic Research, 1964.

Chenery, Hollis, and Clark, Paul G. *Interindustry Economics*. New York: John Wiley & Sons, Inc., 1959.

Eisenstadt, S. N. *Israeli Society*. New York: Basic Books, Inc., 1967.

Evans, Michael K. *An Econometric Model of Part of the Israeli Economy*. Discussion Paper No. 86. Philadelphia: University of Pennsylvania.

Falk Project for Economic Research in Israel. *Fifth Report, 1959 and 1960*. Jerusalem: Jerusalem Post Press, August, 1961.

Gaebelein, Paul W., Jr. "Devaluation Under Full Employment and Inflation: The Case of Israel." Unpublished Ph. D. dissertation, Department of Economics, Claremont Graduate School, 1967.

Haberler, G. M. *A Survey of International Trade Theory*. Special Papers in International Economics, No. 1. Princeton: Princeton University Press, 1961.

Halevi, Nadav. "The Characteristics of Israel's Economic Growth." *Economic Development Issues: Greece, Israel, Taiwan, Thailand*. Supplementary Paper No. 25, issued by the Committee for Economic Development. New York, September, 1968.

_____, and Klinov-Malul, Ruth. *The Economic Development of Israel*. New York: Frederick A. Praeger, Inc., 1968.

Heth, Meir. *Banking Institutions in Israel*. Jerusalem: Maurice Falk Institute for Economic Research in Israel, 1966.

145

Horowitz, David. *The Economics of Israel*. New York: Pergamon Press, 1967.
─────── . "Israel," *World Economic Problems and Policies*. Edited by Herbert Prochnow. New York: Harper and Row, 1965.
Kanovsky, Eliyahu. *The Economic Impact of the Six-Day War*. (Praeger Special Studies in International Economics and Development.) New York: Frederick A. Praeger, Inc., 1970.
Kenen, Peter B. *British Monetary Policy and the Balance of Payments, 1951–1957*. Cambridge: Harvard University Press, 1967.
Kleiman, Ephraim. "The Structure of Israel Manufacturing Industries 1952–1962." Jerusalem: Israel University Press, December, 1964. (mimeographed.)
Mandelbaum, Moshe Yaacov. "The Role of Development Loans Extended by the Israel Government in the Process of Industrialization 1956–1962." Unpublished Ph. D. dissertation, Vanderbilt University, January,1968.
Meade, J. E. *The Theory of International Economic Policy*. Vol 1: *The Balance of Payments*. Cambridge, England: Oxford University Press.
Miernyk, William H. *The Elements of Input-Output Analysis*. New York: Random House, 1967.
Mitchell, Wesley C. *Business Cycles and Their Causes*. Berkeley, California: University of California Press, 1941.
Ofer, Gur. *The Service Industries in a Developing Economy: Israel as a Case Study*. New York: Frederick A. Praeger, Inc., 1967.
Patinkin, Don. *The Israel Economy: The First Decade*. Jerusalem: The Falk Project for Economic Research in Israel, November, 1959.
Pines, David. "Direct Export Subsidies in Israel 1952–1958." Jerusalem: The Falk Project for Economic Research in Israel, 1963.
Rubner, Alex. *The Economy of Israel, A Critical Account of the First Ten Years*. New York: Frederick A. Praeger, Inc., 1960.
Sarnat, Marshall. *Saving and Investment Through Retirement Funds in Israel*. Jerusalem: The Maurice Falk Institute for Economic Research in Israel, July, 1966.
Subotnik, Abraham. *The Development of an Econometric Model for Policy Decision-Making in Israel*. Unpublished Ph. D. dissertation, Cornell University, 1967.
Szereszewski, Robert. *Essays on the Structure of the Jewish Economy in Palestine and Israel*. Jerusalem: The Maurice Falk Institute for Economic Research in Israel, June, 1968.

Journals and Periodicals

Ahiram, E. "Comment on National Policy and Economic Decisions in Israel by Kevin Winch," *Social and Economic Studies*, March, 1963.
Bank Leumi Le-Israel B.M. "Review of Economic Conditions in Israel," Special Issue, July, 1966.
Beham, Miriam, and Kleiman, Ephraim. "The Price of Recession," *The Banking Quarterly* (Hebrew), No. 29, June, 1968.
Ben-Shahar, Haim. "The Structure of Interest Rates, Government Financing and Economic Growth," *Kyklos*, 1967.

Bernstein, E. M. "Strategic Factors in Balance of Payments Adjustment," *International Monetary Fund Staff Papers*, August, 1956.

Chenery, H. B., and Bruno, M. "Development Alternatives in an Open Economy: The Case of Israel," *The Economics Journal*, March, 1962.

Derber, M. "National Wage Policy in Israel 1948–1962," *Quarterly Review of Economics and Business*, Vol. 3, No. 3, Autumn, 1963.

Dun's Review. "Israel: The War-Peace Economy," Vol. 93, No. 4, April, 1969.

Gafni, A., Halevi, N., and Hanoch, G. "Classification of Tariffs by Function," *Kyklos*, XVI, No. 2, 1963.

Halevi, Nadav. "Economic Policy Discussion and Research in Israel," *American Economic Review Supplement*, LIX, No. 4, Part 2, September, 1969.

Horowitz, David. "The New Economic Policy in Israel," *Middle Eastern Affairs*, Vol. 14, No. 6, June/July, 1963.

Houthakker, H. S., and Magee, Stephen P., "Income and Price Elasticities in World Trade," *Review of Economics and Statistics,* LI, May, 1969.

Hovne, Avner. "The Economic Scene in Israel," *Midstream*, Vol. 13, No. 3, April, 1967.

Israel Discount Bank, Ltd. *Business Review.*

Jefferson, C. W., Smas, K. I., and Swann, D. "The Control of Incomes and Prices in the United Kingdom, 1964–1967: Policy and Experience," *The Canadian Journal of Economics,* I, No. 2, May, 1968.

Kleiman, Ephraim. "The Place of Manufacturing in the Growth of the Israel Economy," *The Journal of Development Studies*, Vol. 3, No. 223, April, 1967.

Kreinin, Mordechai E., "Israel and the European Economic Community," *Quarterly Journal of Economics*, LXXXII, May, 1968.

_____. "Israel's Export Problem," *Southern Economic Journal*, XXV, No. 2, October, 1958.

Lipsey, R. G. "The Relation Between Unemployment and the Rate of Change of Money Wage Rates in the United Kingdom, 1862–1957: A Further Analysis," *Economica*, NSXXVII, February, 1960.

Lovasy, Gertrud. "Inflation and Exports in Primary Producing Countries," *International Monetary Fund Staff Papers*, March, 1962.

Lubell, Harold. "The Public and Private Sectors and Investment in Israel," RAND Corporation P–2176, 1961. (Mimeographed.)

McDiarmid, Orville J. "Japan and Israel," *Finance and Development*, Vol. 3, No. 2, June, 1966.

Meyer, A. J. "The Economic Problems of Israel," *Economic Development and Cultural Change*, Vol. 10, No. 331, April, 1962.

Michaely, Michael. "Devaluation, Cost Inflation and the Supply of Exports," *Economia Internazionale* (Italy), IX, No. 1, February, 1956.

_____. "Relative Prices and Income Absorption Approaches to Devaluation: A Partial Reconciliation," *American Economic Review,* L, No. 1, March, 1960.

Phillips, A. W. "The Relation Between Unemployment and the Rate of Change of Money Wage Rates in the United Kingdom, 1861–1957," *Economica*, NSXXV, November, 1958.

Reimer, S. "Israel: Ten Years of Economic Dependence," *Oxford Economic Papers*, XII, June, 1960.

————. "The Devaluation of the Israel Pound," *Kyklos*, XV, No. 3, 1962.
Rosenberg, Leonard G. "Industrial Exports: Israel's Requirement for Self-Support," *Middle East Journal*, Spring, 1958.
Smithies, Arthur. "The Balance of Payments and the Classical Medicine," *Review of Economics and Statistics*, XLVI, May, 1964.
Spengler, J. J. "The Economy and Policy of Israel," *Southern Economic Journal*. XVIII. No. 1, July, 1961.
The Israeli Economist. "The Argument Over Unemployment." April, 1967.
————. "What Price a Recession?" March, 1967.
Van Cleef, Eugene. "The Status of Israel — And a Look Ahead," *Middle East Journal*, Summer, 1964.
Winch, K. F. "National Policy and Economic Decisions in Israel," *Social and Economic Studies*, Vol. 11, No. 170, June, 1962.

Newspapers

The Jerusalem Post. 1965–1970.
The Journal of Commerce. (New York) 1967–1970.
The New York Times. February 23, 1969.

Israeli Government Publications

Central Bureau of Statistics. *Labour Force Survey, 1967*. Jerusalem: 1969.
————. *Monthly Bulletin of Statistics*. 1967–1970.
————. *Monthly Foreign Trade Statistics*. 1964–1970.
————. *Statistical Abstract of Israel*. 1956–1968.
————. *Statistical Bulletin of Israel*. 1964–1966.
Economic Planning Authority. *Israel Economic Development, Past Progress and Plan for the Future*. March, 1968.
Ministry of Commerce and Industry, *Israel Economic Forum*. Foerder, Y. "Banking and Capital Markets." August, 1963.
————. Kleir, A. "Raising Efficiency in Industry." May, 1961.
————. Palgi, Y. "Airports and Airlines." December, 1962,
————. Tsur, M. "Improving the Link Between Producer and Consumer." May, 1961.
Ministry of Finance, Pinchas Sapir, *Budget Address, 1966/67*

Bank of Israel Publications

Bank of Israel. *Annual Report*. 1962–1969.
————. *Bulletin*. Barnea, Michael. "The Financial Structure of Israel's Mortgage Banks, 1958–1964." December, 1965.
————. Baruch, Y. "Import Taxes and Export Subsidies in Israel, 1955–1961." 1962.
————. Bregman, Arie. "The Influence of Changes in Investment of Product and Employment in Boom and Slump Periods in Israel (1965–1968)." July, 1970.

_____ . Davidov, Flora. "The Liberalization of Imports — February 1962 to May 1965." April, 1966.

_____ . "Economic Developments in the First Half of 1965." December, 1965.

_____ . "Economic Developments in the First Half of 1966." November, 1966.

_____ . "Input-Output Tables." (Unpublished.) 1963.

_____ . "National Budget for the Fiscal Year 1965/66." March, 1965.

_____ . "National Budget for 1966." April, 1966.

_____ . "Report on the Increase in the Money Supply During the Period Between October 31, 1964 and September 30, 1965." June, 1966.

_____ . Steinberg, Avigdor. "Bill Brokerage in Israel, 1963)1967." March, 1968.

_____ . Tamari, Meir. 'Allocation of Short-Term Bank Credit to Israel's Industrial Companies, 1956/57 — 1963/64." June, 1966.

Other Official Agencies

International Bank for Reconstruction and Development.
International Labor Office. Report to the Government of Israel on Manpower Assessment and Planning. Geneva: 1965.
International Monetary Fund.
    International Financial Statistics. 1966–1970.

Personal Interviews

Arnon, Jacob. Director of the Economic Planning Authority and Director-General of the Israeli Treasury. October, 1969.
Barkai, Haim. The Maurice Falk Institute for Economic Research in Israel. September, 1970.
Bergman, Arthur D. President of the Maritime Bank of Israel. September, 1970.
Bregman, Ari. Economist, Bank of Israel. September, 1970.
Gafne, Simcha. President of the Kupat Am Bank. September, 1970.
Gilshon, Aharon. Senior Economist, Bank of Israel. September, 1970.
Halevi, Nadav. The Maurice Falk Institute for Economic Research in Israel. September, 1970.
Horowitz, David. Governor of the Bank of Israel. October, 1969.
Kahana, Aaron. Executive Vice-President, Israel Discount Bank (New York). April, 1971.
Kleiman, Ephraim. The Maurice Falk Institute for Economic Research in Israel. Personal Correspondence. September, 1970.
Ronall, Joachim O. Federal Reserve Bank of New York. October, 1968.
Schwartz, David. Treasury of the Government of Israel. Numerous occasions, 1968–1971.
Sheffer, Eliezer. Director of Research, Bank of Israel. March, 1969 and September, 1970.
Yoran, Joseph. Economist, Bank of Israel. September, 1970.

INDEX

Note: c = chart; n = footnote; t = table.

ALLON, Yigal, 116, 118
American Trade and Industrial
   Development with Israel, Inc., 58

BALANCE of payments *see* Balance
   of trade
Balance of trade: 26-7, 61, 67t, 68,
   97, 141; current account, 9, 25;
   deficit, 9, 122, 136; methods of
   adjustment, 3-8; policy, 5-6, 10,
   14-15, 25, 37; *see also* Exports;
   Import surplus; Imports
Bank of Israel: 17-21, 38-40, 60-1,
   124, 142-4; anti-inflationary policy,
   25-6, 28, 66; balance of payments
   policy, 5, 10; bonds, 9, 10; and
   construction sector, 82, 84, 87;
   financing government deficit, 17,
   40, 55; restrictive measures by,
   28-32, 51-5, 110, 141; *see also*
   Credit; Foreign currency assets;
   Interest rates; Money supply;
   Open-market operations;
   Rediscount rates; Reserve requirements; Sàvings deposits
Banks: commercial, 18-21, 31, 51,
   54, 55, 82; public mortgage, 82; *see
   also* Bank of Israel
Barkai, Haim, 140-1, 142, 144
Barnea, Michael, 82
Beham, Miriam, 140
Bill brokerage, 20, 20t, 32, 32t, 40,
   50, 51t, 110
Budget: 32-8 *passim*, 59-60, 104t,
   133; deficit, 13t, 14, 17, 33, 34t,
   35, 37, 40, 55-7, 56t, 59-60, 68,
   135; development, 12, 14, 15, 18,
   25, 33, 34t, 35, 45, 56t, 57, 101,
   102, 103-5, 104t, 106t; fiscal years:
   1964/5, 33, 34t; 1965/6, 33-5, 34t,
   131; 1966/7, 35-6, 78, 103-4;
   1967/8, 37-8, 55-7, 56t; 1968/9,
   56t, 57, 59; 1969/70, 56t, 57,
   59-60; government borrowing, 12,
   13t, 14, 17, 33, 37, 39t, 40, 59-60;
   government loans, 106t, 107t;

receipts, 12-14, 13t, 33, 34t, 105;
   recession policy, 26, 32-5; struc-
   ture, 12-14, 13t; *see also* Bank of
   Israel, financing government deficit;
   Defense expenditures; Government;
   Investment, public; Taxation

CAPITAL inflow: 5, 9, 10, 12, 26, 28,
   33, 38, 39t, 51, 52t, 54, 59, 105,
   106t, 110, 129, 135, 140; *see also*
   Foreign currency assets
Cartels, 27, 100-1
Collective bargaining *see* Histradrut
Consumer Price Index *see* Prices
Construction: 36, 41; commercial and
   industrial, 71, 107-8, 109c, 112;
   economic policy, 32, 37, 77, 78,
   82, 85, 103-5, 104t, 108; inputs
   from other sectors, 88-93, 90-3t,
   118; investment, 77-8, 85, 85t, 86c,
   88, 112; residential, 77-95, 116,
   134; public, 32, 37, 103-5; *see also*
   Bank of Israel, and construction
   sector; Employment and unemployment, construction sector; Housing;
   Wages, construction sector
Consumption, 6, 26, 36, 60, 112, 120,
   121t, 129-30, 133-4, 135-6, 141
Cost-of-living allowance, 7, 17, 26, 36,
   59, 84, 102, 107, 110, 129-34
   passim, 138, 142; *see also* Wages
Credit: 17, 18-21, 20t, 28, 33, 35,
   38-40, 39t, 51-4, 52t, 53t; to construction sector, 82, 84; directed, 18,
   19t, 28, 29t, 31, 105, 110; for
   exporters, 20-1; *see also* Bill
   brokerage

DEFENSE expenditures: 55, 57, 122;
   bonds, 55, 60; exports, 118;
   imports, 26, 71, 140; loans, 136;
   production, 118, 121; *see also*
   Six-Day War
Deficit *see* Bank of Israel, financing
   government deficit; Budget, deficit

151

Deflation *see* Inflation and deflation
Devaluation: 4-8, 9, 32, 37, 78, 98,
  102, 141-2; effects of cost-of-living
  on, 6-7, 17; November 1967, 27,
  57, 66, 71, 116, 125, 135
Development budget *see* Budget,
  development
Diamond industry, 8, 27, 45, 67, 125

ECONOMIC dependence, 25, 67t, 68,
  97
Employment and unemployment: 36,
  44c, 45, 88-9, 92t, 95n, 98, 102,
  110-19 *passim*, 119c, 130-2 *passim*;
  construction sector, 84, 85t, 86c,
  112; Employment Headquarters,
  133; and exports, 66-7; policy,
  36-7, 49, 116, 118, 133, 142-3; and
  prices, 7, 116, 130, 133, 136;
  unemployment insurance, 133,
  134, 139n; *see also* Industrial
  production, productivity
Eshkol, Levi, 129, 131
Evans, Michael K., 8, 66, 129-30
Exchange rate, 16, 61, 66, 141; *see
  also* Devaluation
Export Funds, 19t, 20, 31
Exports: 18, 27, 41, 45-9, 61-71, 92t,
  98, 108-9, 113, 114, 118, 120t,
  121, 122, 124-5, 126c, 134, 141,
  144; comparison with other
  countries, 14, 14t; costs included in
  expanding, 45, 49; effects on
  recession, 25-6, 27, 61, 63-8;
  financing, 20, 31; industrial, 8, 45,
  46t, 48c, 61, 64c, 84-5, 97-8,
  101-2, 140; policy, 3, 20, 26, 35,
  49, 66-8, 77, 96; promotion, 57-9,
  101; of services, 27n, 68-71, 69t,
  70t; subsidies, 7-8, 9, 15, 37, 49,
  66, 101, 112, 141; trends, 27, 46t,
  47c, 48c, 61, 63-8, 63c, 64c, 65t;
  see also Balance of trade

FISCAL policy *see* Budget; Govern-
  ment; Imports, tariffs; Taxation
Foreign currency assets, 21, 38, 39t,
  51, 52t, 54-5, 78, 97; *see also*
  Capital inflow
Foreign trade *see* Balance of trade;
  Exports; Imports

GOVERNMENT: anti-inflationary
  policy, 17, 33, 66, 102-3, 112-13;
construction policy, 78, 82, 84,
  108; and Histradrut, 6, 15-7, 36,
  57, 59, 60, 116, 130, 132-3, 134-5;
  incomes policy, 17, 59, 130-9;
  investment policy, 15, 25, 37, 96;
  recession policy, 5, 9-10, 25-7,
  32-8, 41, 103-4, 140-4; public
  employees, 36-7, 130, 133; service
  imports by, 68, 70t; trade policy,
  9-10, 14-15; 25-7, 57-9, 66-8, 101;
  see also Budget; Devaluation;
  Exports, promotion, subsidies;
  Imports, controls, subsidies, tariffs;
  Taxation
Gross national product, 9, 28, 36, 37,
  79c, 80t, 85t, 86c, 112, 118, 140

HALEVI, Nadav, 14, 98, 140, 143-4
Histradrut: cost-of-living allowance
  policy, 59, 84, 110, 130, 132, 133,
  134-5, employment practices, 103,
  116, 118; structure of, 6-7, 15-7,
  110, 130; wage policy, 33, 36, 57,
  59, 60, 84, 102, 110, 114, 130-3
Horowitz, David, 26, 105, 131-2
Housing: expenditures, 77-8, 84, 87;
  public, 78, 79c, 80t; starts, 78, 83c,
  84, 85; *see also* Construction

IMMIGRATION, 26, 77, 78, 79c, 80t,
  84-5, 87, 107
Import surplus, 9, 25, 28, 61, 65t, 67t,
  102, 129, 140, 144; *see also*
  Balance of trade
Imports: 55, 60-1, 67t, 68, 88, 96-8,
  116, 130, 140; comparison with
  other countries, 14, 14t; consumer
  goods, 41, 44c, 134, 135-6;
  controls, 7, 9, 14-15; dependence of
  production on, 61, 62c, 96-7;
  investment goods, 41, 43c; liberalization policy, 15, 61, 99; recession
  policy, 27, 41; services, 68-71, 69t,
  70t; tariffs, 57, 61, 98-100, 99t,
  102, 112, 134; trends, 41, 42c, 43c,
  61, 65t; *see also* Balance of trade;
  Defense expenditures, imports;
  Economic dependence; Import
  surplus
Income, 84, 87, 105, 129, 134, 135,
  136; *see also* Restitution payments;
  Taxation; Wages
Incomes policy *see* Government,
  incomes policy

152

Industrial production: 41, 43c, 45, 46t, 62c, 89, 92t, 93t, 96-103, 116, 118-26, 119c, 120t; economic development, 121-5, 123c, 124-5t; productivity, 98, 99-100, 102, 110-12, 111c, 118, 130, 132-3; *see also* Exports, industrial; Imports, dependence of production on
Inflation and deflation: 3-8, 9, 57, 102-3, 107-8, 129-34 *passim*, 138-9, 142-4; devaluation and, 4-5, 9, 17, 102; exports and, 45, 49, 112-13, 141; inflationary government-ment policies, 14, 17; wage policy and, 7, 17, 33, 102, 130; *see also* Bank of Israel, anti-inflationary policy; Cost-of-living allowance; Government, anti-inflationary policy, incomes policy; Prices
Interest rates, 5, 18, 20, 32, 40, 110
Investment: 9, 35, 87, 98, 101, 105, 107-12, 108t; foreign, 10, 37, 110; Law for Encouragement of, 38, 101; manufacturing, 96, 102, 105, 107, 112; public, 78, 103-5, 104t; real estate speculation, 32, 77, 78, 82, 107, 110; *see also* Budget, development; Construction; Government, investment policy

JERUSALEM Economic Conference, 58
Jewish Agency, 12, 37, 54, 59, 106t, 133, 141

KANOVSKY, Eliyahu, 38, 58
Kleiman, Ephraim, 140-1, 142
Klinov-Mahul, Ruth, 14

LABOR costs, 49, 100, 102, 105, 110-12, 111c, 113t, 114, 114t; *see also* Industrial production, produc-tivity; Wages
Lipsey, R. G., 136
Liquidity ratios *see* Reserve require-ments
Lovasy, Gertrude, 45, 49

MANDELBAUM, Moshe Yaacov, 97
Manufacturers Association, 16, 133
Manufacturing *see* Industrial produc-tion
Mapai, 15, 16, 17
Mapam, 16, 132

Michaely, Michael, 7, 133
Mitun *see* Bank of Israel; Government
Monetary policy *see* Bank of Israel
Money supply, 17, 21, 28-32, 30t, 31t, 38-40, 51-5, 51t, 52t, 102, 110, 142

NATIONAL income *see* Gross national product
National Insurance Institute, 132, 133
New Economic Policy (1962), 9

OPEN-MARKET operations, 18, 29t, 39t, 40, 51-4, 52t, 53t, 55

PATINKIN, Don, 25, 131
Pazak accounts, 21
Phillips, A. W., 136
Prices: 3-4, 114-16, 115c, 117t, 129-30, 135, 136-7, 141; domestic and foreign relative, 3-4, 116, 117t; housing, 84; freeze, 27, 66, 105, 108-9, 113; Price Headquarters, 133; *see also* Bank of Israel, anti-inflationary policy; Govern-ment, anti-inflationary policy; Inflation and deflation
Productivity *see* Industrial production, productivity
Profits, 7, 27, 110-12
Protection *see* Imports, controls, tariffs

REDISCOUNT rates, 20, 29t, 53t, 54, 55
Reparation payments, 9, 10, 12, 25, 105, 106t; *see also* Restitution payments
Reserve requirements, 18, 19t, 28, 29t, 31, 38, 40, 53t, 54, 110
Restitution payments, 9, 10, 21, 26, 32, 36, 77-8, 87, 107, 133, 134, 141; *see also* Reparation payments
Rosenberg, Leonard G., 97

SAPIR, Pinchas, 10, 84, 130, 132
Savings deposits, 18, 21
Sheffer, Eliezer, 141
Six-Day War, 26, 38, 41, 51, 55, 57, 66, 71, 134, 136, 138
Smithies, Arthur, 7
Subotnik, Abraham, 6, 8, 66
Subsidies: 16, 32; prices, 131, 133; *see also* Exports, subsidies

153

TAMAN accounts, 21
  Tariffs *see* Imports, tariffs
Taxation: 22n, 32, 33, 36, 131, 133,
  135; corporate, 101; indirect, 17,
  35, 36, 60, 131; personal income,
  17, 35, 55, 100, 136, 143-44
Tourism, 27n, 70t, 71

VAN CLEEF, Eugene, 97
Volunteers for Israel Products, 57-8

WAGES: 3, 6, 7, 16-17, 33, 36, 49,
  88-9, 92t, 100, 102, 105, 110,
  111c, 112-14, 113t, 129-34 *passim*,
  136-8, 137t, 142-4; construction
  sector, 84; public employees, 16-17,
  33, 130, 131; wage freeze, 27, 59,
  66, 105, 108-9, 113, 114, 130, 133,
  134; *see also* Histradrut